Study Guide for Teachers

High Class Natives
The Ballroom Dancers & Mbira Players
By Alf E.F. Muronda

Zimbabwe Secondary Schools
A Level English Literature Drama
Set Book

Acknowledge

High Class Natives – The Ballroom Dancers & Mbira Players is a project inspired by the unsung heroes of the 1st & 2nd Chimurenga. Even though the book carries the name of its authour, it is the work of the many whose names remain invisible on the printed page.

This *Study Guide for Teachers* is a product of the research and writing by Imbuwa Mubiana Aongola, Alf E.F. Muronda, and the guiding spirit of Professor Beverly Robinson.

ISBN 978-1-965398-06-7

Table of Contents

PREFACE

Welcome to the *Study Guide for Teachers*, for *High Class Natives – The Ballroom Dancers & Mbira Players*, a Zimbabwe Secondary School A Level Literature drama set book.

This guide is designed to help educators effectively teach the play and engage students in meaningful discussions and analyses. The play tells its story through various themes, character development, and cultural conflicts that provide valuable learning opportunities for students.

The play, centered around the Choto family, is set against the backdrop of the war of liberation in Rhodesia (now Zimbabwe), capturing the economic, socio-political dynamics and the impact of the conflict on African families in the countryside and the townships of Salisbury (now Harare). Through its complex characters and evocative narrative, the play explores themes of cultural assimilation, family obligations, and the struggle for identity in a changing world.

Dramatic Techniques

The play employs several dramatic techniques to enhance the storytelling and convey the themes of the story effectively:

- Symbolism: The contrast between African mbira music and European classical ballroom dancing music symbolizes the cultural conflict between traditional African values and European assimilation.
- Characterization: Multi-dimensional characters with distinct personalities, backgrounds, and motivations allow students to explore various perspectives in a country that was in political turmoil and social distress.
- Conflict: Both cultural and political conflicts within one family drive the narrative, highlighting the tension between

traditional African values and the desire for European assimilation.

- Flashbacks: The use of flashbacks reveals the characters' past experiences and traumas, providing context for their actions and motivations.
- Dialogue: Authentic conversations in the characters' native Shona language and English convey the characters' emotions, thoughts, and cultural backgrounds, reflecting the complexities of their relationships.
- Setting: The contrasting environments of a rural village community life and the insular urban life in Beatrice Cottages underscore the impact of the war and displacement experienced by the characters.
- Symbolic Actions: Actions such as Sally's avid participation in ballroom dancing symbolize her desire to assimilate into European culture and distance herself from her African heritage.
- Themes: The play explores themes of cultural assimilation, family obligations, social status, and political and social change.

Learning Objectives

The play is composed of 9 Acts in 16 scenes. The guide provides a detailed summary of each of the 16 scenes. Each scene represents a learning unit. By the end of the unit, students should be able to:

- Analyze Character Development: Identify and explain the development of the main characters throughout the play, including their motivations, conflicts, and relationships.
- Interpret Themes: Discuss the central themes of the play and provide examples from the text to support their interpretations.
- Evaluate Literary Devices: Recognize and analyze the use of literary devices such as symbolism, foreshadowing, and irony, and explain their significance in the play.

- <u>Engage in Critical Discussions</u>: Participate in group discussions, expressing their ideas clearly and respectfully while considering different perspectives.
- <u>Write Analytical Essays</u>: Compose well-organized and coherent essays that analyze specific aspects of the play, supported by textual evidence.

These objectives ensure that students not only understand the content of the play but also develop critical thinking and analytical skills. We hope this guide provides educators with the tools and insights needed to facilitate a rich and engaging learning experience for their students.

INTRODUCTION

OVERVIEW OF THE PLAY

The play is a poignant slice of life set in Rhodesia circa 1977, unfolding over a four-month period. It centers around the Choto family, who reside in the Beatrice Cottages enclave, a relatively upscale area compared to the sprawling National African Township where the rest of the African population of what was then known as Harare lived. (*Salisbury became Harare and Harare became Mbare after independence in 1980.*) The narrative delves into the lives of the recently widowed patriarch, Majasi, his successful son Rwizi, and Rwizi's wife, Sally, as they navigate the complexities of family, culture, and societal expectations.

The backdrop of the play is the war of liberation raging in the Rhodesian countryside, which has upended the lives of the African population living in the villages. While no place in Rhodesia is entirely safe from the war, the city offers relative safety. This is why Majasi, the recently widowed patriarch of the Choto family, finds himself living in his son (Rwizi)'s house in Beatrice Cottages. His own home in Mhondoro was burned down by Rhodesian Army soldiers after they killed his wife for cooking a meal for guerrilla fighters.

Rwizi has naturally taken on the responsibility of caring for his elderly, infirm father, Majasi, and his 18-year-old brother, Andrew, a mbira-playing virtuoso. Andrew is an intelligent young man who has completed Form Four but has no prospects for work or further education in a country reeling under UN economic sanctions and the ravages of war.

Despite his meager means, Majasi, a traditional Shona African father, had made provisions for his family's well-being by investing in his son's education. He sold his small herd of cattle to pay for Rwizi's university education, enabling Rwizi to secure a coveted management position with the City of Salisbury Revenue Department. In Shona tradition, the eldest son is expected to care for his younger siblings and aging parents. Thus, Majasi and Andrew's presence in Rwizi's life should be seen as an expected extension of his responsibilities.

However, Rwizi's wife, Sally, an orphan with no family ties or obligations, has different priorities. She is determined to raise their 6-year-old son, John, to be a European-cultured person who does not speak Shona. To that end, they have enrolled John in an exclusive, expensive white school, and Sally insists that only English be spoken in their home. Sally's lack of empathy and rejection of her African heritage stem from her traumatic childhood, where her mother was raped by her own father and subsequently blamed and ostracized by their village. As an adult, Sally has mentally cut herself off from her mother's family.

Sally has figuratively built a wall around her life and their Beatrice Cottages home to keep out mbira music and other aspects of African culture. Inside her home, she aspires to all things European, including her avid participation in a European classical music ballroom dancing club. This affiliation reflects the choices she has made to distance herself from her African roots.

The war forces Sally and Rwizi to accommodate Rwizi's family, a family whose African culture and values are antithetical to everything Sally aspires to be as a modern Euro-African person. This tension between tradition and modernity, family obligations, and cultural identity forms the crux of the play's narrative.

THEMES

1. <u>Cultural Assimilation and Identity</u>: The play explores the tension between traditional African values and the desire to assimilate into European culture. Sally's determination to raise her son with European values and her disdain for African traditions highlight the struggles of cultural assimilation and the impact on personal identity.

2. <u>Family Obligations and Loyalty</u>: The play examines the responsibilities and duties within a family, particularly the expectations placed on the eldest son, Rwizi, to care for his relatives. This theme is juxtaposed with Sally's desire to maintain a nuclear family and her resistance to accommodating her in-laws.
3. <u>Social Status and Class</u>: The Choto family's social standing and their aspirations for a higher status (high class natives) are central to the narrative. The play highlights the pressures and sacrifices made to achieve and maintain social status, as seen in Sally's obsession with ballroom dancing and hosting sophisticated parties.
4. <u>Political and Social Change</u>: Set against the backdrop of the Zimbabwe war for independence, the play addresses the broader socio-political dynamics of the time. Rwizi's clandestine support for the liberation movements and the impact of war on the family's life underscore the theme of political and social change.

RELEVANCE

The play is a significant window into the lives of African families during a tumultuous period in Zimbabwean history. It captures the complexities of cultural assimilation, the challenges of balancing tradition with modernity, and the impact of socio-political changes on personal lives. Through its complex characterizations and evocative language, the play offers a nuanced portrayal of the struggles and aspirations of the Choto family, making it a compelling and thought-provoking piece of literature of this time period.

Chapter 1

STORY & AUTHOUR'S BACKGROUND INFORMATION

HISTORICAL CONTEXT

To fully appreciate the social and economic conditions that the Choto family faces, students will first have to have a basic understanding of the country's history. It is crucial to understand how the country became a British colony and the rise of Ian Smith and his cohorts, who sought to control the country and its resources under a white minority regime in perpetuity at the expense of the African majority.

Students should be familiar with key historical events, starting with Cecil John Rhodes's Pioneer Column hoisting the British Union Jack flag in 1890 at what was then called Fort Salisbury, marking the beginning of British control over Zimbabwe, which they named Rhodesia.

Additionally, students should have knowledge of the liberation war known as the Second Chimurenga, which began in 1965 and ended in 1979. This war led and organized by the indigenous Africans themselves through the Zimbabwe African People's Union (ZAPU) and Zimbabwe African National Union (ZANU) aimed to dismantle the institutionalized discrimination and oppression of the African population, a legacy of the Pioneer Column. Understanding these historical contexts will provide students with a deeper insight into the challenges and dynamics faced by the Choto family.

SOCIAL CONTEXT

The administration of Rhodesia under racially biased entrenched laws led to the uprising of the oppressed African population. The brutal war between the Rhodesian Government army and the ZIPRA/ZANLA forces, primarily fought in the countryside, left the rural population living in a state of siege. An economy that had brought prosperity to the white minority population and deprivation to the African majority population in the rural areas had all but ceased functioning. Surviving in the farms and villages in the rural areas became tenuous because of land mines, active battles between the opposing forces and numbing fear of what's going to blow up next. Continuing losses at the hands of the guerrilla forces led the government to propose and enact draconian measures including building camps known as KEEPS where they herded villagers into high-wired-fenced camps to prevent collaboration between the villagers and the freedom fighters. Those who could escape sought refuge with families in the African townships in Salisbury, such as the Choto family, or became homeless, living and sleeping wherever they could in the streets of the townships.

Understanding the conflicts and motivations that drive a character in any story requires one to have a point of reference and knowledge of the time and place where the action takes place. In the play, *High Class Natives*, knowledge and familiarity with the conditions prevailing in the African population in the Rhodesia of 1977 is a must for students studying the play. 1977 was the height of the war which would end in 1979 with the people's guerrilla forces' victory over the Rhodesia Government army. The living conditions and the human cost of that military victory serve as the backdrop of the play.

In summary here are key aspects of the social conditions the Choto family and the African population of that time lived under:

1. Economic Inequality: The 1970s, Africans experienced significant economic disparities compared to the white minority and other minority racial groups in the country. Young African people like Andrew had limited or no employment opportunities, unlike their counterparts in the white, Indian, and Coloured communities. The economy was dominated by the white minority, who controlled all agricultural and key industries, leaving the black majority with few opportunities for economic advancement.

2. Political Oppression: The Rhodesian government, led by Ian Smith, maintained white minority rule and resisted negotiations for a democratic political system. Failure to negotiate resulted in an all-out push for black majority governance. The push for majority rule led to widespread government oppression of the African population which led to the protracted guerrilla war fought between African nationalist forces and the Rhodesian security forces.

3. Displacement and Violence: The war of liberation caused significant displacement and violence in the countryside. Many African villages were destroyed, and families were uprooted, as seen with Majasi's village being burned down and his wife being killed by Rhodesian Army soldiers. However, violence also occurred in the African townships. Those suspected of opposing African nationalist goals of black majority rule, like Sally, faced violent punishment from the African community. Individuals were beaten, houses were petrol-bombed, and cars were damaged with rocks and slashed tires.

4. Social Isolation: Those who sought refuge in the townships were not always welcomed by the larger community, even if they were with their own blood families. In many instances, they experienced social isolation and a lack of community support. This is evident in the play when Chaitezvi laments the absence of neighbourly help in the city compared to the village.

5. Cultural/Political Conflict: Although the racial apartheid legislation and economic management of the country were clearly oppressive and detrimental to the majority of the African population's interests, not all Africans favored the political change advocated by the majority. Sally, in the play, represents those who were not aggrieved by white minority rule. The symbolism of the African mbira and its music, contrasted with European classical ballroom dancing music, highlights the cultural and political conflict in the play. Mbira music represents freedom before the advent of Europeans and the colonization of the country. It stands for African

tradition, language, extended family, and community, while European classical music embodies a different nuclear family cultural identity. These two genres serve as instruments of cultural and political conflict, each representing a way of life that may be antithetical to the other. The central question for Africans at the time was whether one could embrace both cultures or had to choose one over the other. Unlike Sally, who made a clear-cut decision to adopt European culture, Rwizi embodies the cultural conflict experienced by the majority, torn between tradition and an eclectic inclusion of the other.

6. <u>Education and Employment</u>: By the 1970s, the promise of education as a key to employment and economic success for Africans had already proven to be an illusion. Despite assurances, the racist system kept Africans from meaningful economic participation. The African majority took up arms against Ian Smith's regime when it became clear that education alone would not overcome racial barriers. Andrew and his friends, despite their intelligence and education, could not find employment. Before the war, they might have secured low-level clerk jobs, but even those opportunities vanished with the conflict.

Overall, the social conditions for Africans in Rhodesia during this period were characterized by economic hardship, political oppression, displacement, social isolation, cultural conflict, and limited opportunities for advancement. The play is driven by how these challenges impacted the lives of the Choto family and their community.

Authour's Biography: Alf E.F. Muronda

Alf E.F. Muronda has had a varied career in the creative arts industry. He holds a Master of Fine Arts degree in writing, film, and television. His body of work includes poetry, novels, screenplays, and stage plays, primarily focusing on African culture as it encounters external and internal forces that seek to ignore or discount it.

Born in 1951 in National Township, Salisbury (now Harare), when Zimbabwe was known as Southern Rhodesia, Alf experienced firsthand the challenges faced by the African population. At the time of his birth, there was a severe housing shortage for Africans migrating to Salisbury, the commercial center of the British colony. His father's generation was forced to leave their rural homes due to restrictive colonial policies that limited land and cattle ownership for Africans. These measures were designed to compel Africans, especially men, to work as laborers and clerks for the white population.

Despite the colonial government's reliance on African labor, it made no appropriate preparations for the workforce it was forcibly recruiting. Consequently, the housing in what became known as "African locations" consisted of uniform matchbox dwellings, intended to discourage Africans from viewing their urban residences as permanent homes. These houses were meant to be temporary accommodations while employed by white people, with the expectation that Africans would return to their rural homes once their employment ended.

"High Class Natives" was born from Muronda's childhood memories when his family moved from a matchbox house in National African Township to Beatrice Cottages. At the age of eight, he encountered a new world filled with diverse characters, which inspired the amalgamation of personalities in his play. Creative license allowed him to craft a character like Sally, who was determined to raise a son who could only speak English in a world where everyone else spoke Shona. While that was certainly an extreme situation, there were some quixotic assimilation behaviours among some of the *nouveau riche* African families in Beatrice Cottages as pointed out by his parents that inspired "High Class Natives."

Except From Alf Muronda's unpublished memoir: *"Born Location"*

"**…**My generation's place in our country's history is that we were the first generation to be born in the designated African urban areas after the advent of *varungu (*white people*)*. For that fact, our fellow Africans from the villages labeled us the "*born-locations*". It is a derogative term implying that we, the children born in the hodgepodge of government designated urban locations, did not have the benefit of proper breeding as our village born tribal cousins presumably had. Also implicit in the derogation is the undeniable fact that back then most, if not all of us, were born in squalid conditions. *(Although I was not born in the "Old Bricks" described here I was old enough to know about them.)* Some of us were literally born in structures that had no walls excepting the cloth hung around four wooden poles that designated it as a house. The Old Bricks location was the worst; three or four families were stuck in a room measuring about twenty feet by twenty-five feet, with no partition for individual family privacy other than some kind of curtain hung on a string. There were no cooking facilities; each family had its own paraffin primus stove. In the middle of each of the unplastered bare brick walls of the room were holes that served as windows. The floors were just as rough and bare, hence the name 'Old Bricks'. When one moved into one of these one-room "houses", the empty open space was all there was. I do not remember the exact number they were in each block but I do remember that these one-roomed barn-like multi-family houses were strung in blocks, each block standing about fifteen feet apart from the next one. One of the most dreadful marks against this location was that sometimes on hot days, dark glistening flies buzzed out of the communal toilets that were thrown in between the blocks of the one-roomed houses. These horrible flies, a by-product of the overflowing buckets of human waste, flew in and out in the air around these disease infested toilet buildings.

We moved to what was called the 'Italian Section', later known as Beatrice Road Cottages, which was located on the western fridges of the National African location. It was an enclave of seventy houses separated from the African location by underdeveloped land and a ten-foot barbed wire fence with two gates. The roads in the 'Italian Section' were tarred and the houses had electricity. There was a clubhouse and open spaces for sports. All the houses were single family brick-built three and four bedroom homes with plastered walls and white painted ceiling tiles which made the rooms seem bigger and brighter. Our old semi-detached house in National had no ceiling, the wooden trusses holding up the bare asbestos roof ran between the two adjoining houses with tiny air spaces in between the wood and the brick that carried the louder conversations in one house to the other. Compared to the houses in National, Old Bricks and New Lines, our new 'Italian Section' home was a fairy tale dream house complete with a very fruitful mulberry tree, surrounded by open ground for a front yard lawn, a parking bay for my father's car, a vegetable garden in the back and an empty dirt space by the kitchen where we could play while mother was cooking and watching over us. We had lucked out because none of these accommodations had ever been intended by the government for an African family to occupy.

For several years, the houses in the Italian Section had been lying vacant because those for whom the government had built them had left. Apparently the 'Italian Section' had been a World War II internment camp for potential European fascist sympathizers, their families and possibly Mussolini's Italian soldiers who may have been held as prisoners of war in our country. At the time we did not know where these European families or Italians soldiers had come from and I assume, my father being just so happy and grateful to get the house, did not care to know. However, later when studying history lessons in secondary school, I learned that the Second World War did not include our country, Southern Rhodesia, as one of its theatres. So, I can only speculate that Churchill in the fog of the smoke from his fat cigar had blindly pointed on the map of the British Empire and ordered that his enemies, their families and soldiers of European fascism, be dumped in comfort, among us Africans."

Chapter 2

LITERARY SIGNIFICANCE OF THE PLAY

Given the situation out of which the play was born, the play may hold significant importance in both Zimbabwean and world literature for several reasons:

Significance in Zimbabwean Literature

1. Historical Context: The play provides a vivid portrayal of life in Rhodesia during the war of liberation, capturing the socio-political dynamics and the impact of the conflict on African families. It serves as a historical document that sheds light on the struggles and resilience of the African population during this tumultuous period.
2. Cultural Identity: The play explores the tension between traditional African values and the desire to assimilate into European culture. This theme may resonate with Zimbabwean audiences, reflecting the complexities of cultural identity and the challenges of balancing tradition with modernity.
3. Social Commentary: Through its characters and narrative, the play offers a critique of the social and economic inequalities faced by Africans under white minority rule. It highlights the impact of colonialism and the fight for independence, making it a legitimate piece of social commentary.

Significance in World Literature

1. Universal Themes: The play addresses universal themes such as family obligations, cultural assimilation, and the quest for identity. These themes are relatable to audiences worldwide, making the play relevant beyond its specific historical and geographical context.
2. Representation of African Voices: The play contributes to the representation of African voices in world literature, providing a platform for African stories and perspectives. It enriches the

global literary landscape by offering insights into the experiences and struggles of African communities.

3. <u>Educational Value</u>: The play serves as an educational tool, helping readers and audiences understand the historical and cultural context of Zimbabwe's liberation struggle. It fosters a deeper appreciation of the complexities of decolonization and the impact of colonialism on African societies.

Impact on Culture and Society

1. <u>Cultural Preservation</u>: By incorporating traditional African elements such as mbira music and Shona customs, the play helps preserve and promote African cultural heritage. It encourages a sense of pride and identity among Zimbabwean audiences.

2. <u>Social Awareness</u>: The play raises awareness about the historical injustices and challenges faced by African population. It prompts discussions about social justice, equality, and the importance of cultural heritage.

3. <u>Inspiration for Change</u>: The play's portrayal of resilience and resistance against oppression can inspire contemporary audiences to advocate for social and political change. It serves as a reminder of the cost of liberty and the importance of standing up against tyranny.

Thus, the play may contribute to both Zimbabwean and world literature as it offers valuable insights into the historical and cultural context of Rhodesia. It also addresses universal themes that resonate with audiences globally. It is a proponent of cultural preservation, social awareness, and an inspiration for change for the underdog.

Chapter 3

PLOT STRUCTURE OF THE PLAY

Exposition

<u>Setting and Introduction of Characters:</u>

- The play is set in Beatrice Cottages – an African township in Salisbury, Rhodesia circa1977 at the height of the ongoing liberation war. The war has driven Majasi, the patriarch of the Choto family to flee from his burnt down rural village home to the seek refuge in his eldest son's home (Rwizi) in Beatrice Cottages.
- The main characters, Sally, Rwizi, Majasi, Andrew, John and Belinda are introduced.
- Sally & Rwizi are introduced as avid European classical music ballroom dance club members. There are a middle-class African couple. The wife has aspirations for an exclusive nuclear type family lifestyle. Their 6-year-old son John is introduced as being raised by Sally to be a European cultured person who only speaks English evidenced by Sally chastising the boy for speaking to his grandfather (Majasi) in Shona.
- Old Majasi loves and listens to mbira music, (which is hated by Sally) on the radio.
- Belinda, Sally's best friend is a traditional African woman who, like Majasi, loves mbira music.
- Andrew, Rwizi's younger brother, a mbira music virtuoso player, has just completed Form Four. He is looking for employment.
- Unlike his wife who overtly opposes majority rule, Rwizi who is a clandestine supporter of African nationalism. He begs off from attending a scheduled ballroom dancing rehearsal with Sally to attend a political meeting (disguised as a bira) with Andrew.
- The arrival of Rwizi's family (Majasi and Andrew) disrupts Rwizi and Sally's carefully manicured life.

Rising Action

Conflict Development:

- Sally's disdain for Rwizi's relatives and her insistence on maintaining an urban non-traditional African nuclear family lifestyle that excludes Rwizi's relatives creates tension. The cultural clash between Sally's European aspirations, Andrew's political sympathies and Majasi's traditional African values intensifies.
- Andrew shares his struggles with unemployment and police harassment, highlighting the economic challenges faced by young Africans. His friends, Chamu and Muchazo, invite him to join their mbira band, adding to the rising tension.
- Sally's obsession with hosting the upcoming ballroom dancing competition after-party and her ultimatum to Rwizi to find alternative accommodation for his father heighten the stakes.

- Sally's decision to force Rwizi to place his father, Majasi, in an old people's home in Plumtree escalates the tension and conflict.

- The worsening economy, the involvement of young people in the liberation struggle, and the social isolation faced by characters like Chaitezvi add to the rising action.
- Andrew confronts Rwizi in his office, demanding to know where their father is. The revelation that Majasi has been placed in an old people's home in Plumtree leads to a heated confrontation and Andrew's declaration that they are no longer brothers continues to rise the action.
- Andrew decides to join the guerrilla fighters when he finds his father dead in Plumtree adding further to the rising action..

Climax

<u>Majasi's Death – Sally's Party</u>

- The climax occurs during Sally's ballroom dancers' championship party when Andrew arrives with the news that their father, Majasi, has died.
- The altercation between Sally and Andrew over Andrew's presence at Sally's party leads to Sally pushing Andrew and Andrew losing his balance. As Andrew falls to the ground the bomb in the bag he is holding could go off and blow them all away.
- The revelation that Sally knew about Majasi's death but chose not to inform Rwizi to avoid spoiling her party shocks Rwizi leading to immediate separation.

Falling Action

- Guilt-ridden and devastated, Rwizi collapses in tears and decides to leave the party with John and Andrew to bury his father.
- Sally's attempts to blame Andrew and continue the party, but it is futile. All the guests except Belinda & Sam immediately abandon the party.
- Sally did not want Majasi in her house so she could have a party with her friends, ironically Majasi, who was not at the party, has stopped Sally's party because Sally's guests all leave when they find out that Majasi is dead.

Resolution

- As Sally sits alone, cradling the ballroom dancing trophy, Belinda points out her (Sally)'s moral failure to her. Sally realizes the consequences of her actions.
- Sally realizes that her actions could lead to the destruction of her family.
- Belinda advises Sally to save her marriage by throwing away the trophy where Rwizi will never see it again and apologize to Rwizi before he buries his father and their marriage.

- The resolution involves the major characters coming to terms with their actions and the need for reconciliation.
- Rwizi comes to terms with his failure in abandoning his filial duty and asks forgiveness from father and mother.
- Sally marks her contrition by following Belinda's advice and goes to Plumtree to support Rwizi, indicating a potential path towards healing and unity within the family.

These elements of the plot drive the narrative and underscore the broader themes of cultural identity, family obligations, emotional turmoil, and the struggle for social and political change.

Note Well

The book *"High Class Natives, The Ballroom Dancers & Mbira Players"* is uniquely arranged with the synopsis placed before the play itself. This is an unusual arrangement, as most stage and screen plays do not include a detailed synopsis of the story they tell.

The authour decided to place the synopsis at the beginning to encourage everyone, especially those unfamiliar with the stage play format, to understand the story and discover its nuances as they read the play.

Educators teaching *"High Class Natives, The Ballroom Dancers & Mbira Players"* are advised to have their students read the synopsis before delving into the lesson units. This approach will make the learning process enjoyable for both students and teachers.

CHAPTER 4

LEARNING UNITS

LESSON PLANS

These lesson plans aim to foster critical thinking, empathy, and a greater appreciation for the complexities of the characters' relationships and the cultural context in which they live. There are 16 lesson units. **Each scene in each act is a lesson unit.** Each of the 16 scenes has been summarized for the educator and broken down with lesson objectives, activities and questions. Students should be assigned specific sections of the play to read before the lesson. Questions are designed to stimulate critical thinking and discussion.

By engaging in these activities and discussions, students will gain a deeper understanding of the characters, themes, and conflicts in the play.

It cannot be emphasized enough that students should be assigned specific relevant scene/s to read from the book before class discussions of the unit.

OCT ONE   Lesson Plan - Scene 1

Scene 1   SUMMARY**:** The play opens in the living room. The scene introduces the friendship between Majasi and his grandson John, who is trying to speak in Shona, so his grandfather can understand a story he is trying to tell him. Sally enters the scene and immediately shows her disregard for Majasi by chastising John for speaking Shona and responding dismissively to Majasi's greeting. Traditionally, a daughter-in-law sits down or curtsy and then greets her father-in-law respectfully by clapping her hands, but Sally disregards this custom.

Scene 1 Lesson Objectives

- <u>Understand Character Relationships</u>: Students will analyze the relationships between Majasi, John, and Sally.
- <u>Explore Themes</u>: Students will discuss themes of language, respect, and cultural identity.

Discussion Questions

1. **Character Relationships**:
   - How does John's attempt to speak Shona to his grandfather reflect their relationship?
   - What does Sally's reaction to John speaking Shona reveal about her character and her relationship with Majasi?
2. **Themes**:
   - How does the scene explore the theme of language and cultural identity? Why is it significant that John tries to speak Shona to his grandfather?
   - What does Sally's disregard for traditional customs reveal about her views on cultural identity and respect?
3. **Conflict and Resolution**:
   - How does Sally's reaction to Majasi's greeting impact the dynamics of the family?
4. **Personal Reflection**:
   - How do the characters' actions and decisions in this scene set the stage for future conflicts in the play?

NOTES

OCT ONE   Lesson Plan - Scene 2

Scene 2

SUMMARY: John follows his mother to her bedroom, where they talk as Sally changes from her work uniform to casual wear. John asks why he can't speak Shona to his grandfather, who, he thinks, doesn't understand English. Sally responds saying the Shona language is for "kaffirs and monkeys" and makes John repeat, "I am not a monkey. I will not speak Shona," rewarding him with sweets afterward.

The conversation between Sally and John is interrupted by a knock at the door, which John answers. Belinda, Sally's best friend and a fellow nurse-matron at the African General Hospital, has come to return Sally's umbrella. When Belinda enters, she respectfully greets Majasi by clapping her hands as custom requires and sits down. Her respectful interaction with Majasi contrasts sharply with Sally's disrespectful behavior. The conversation between Majasi and Belinda also introduces mbira music as a common interest between them.

Scene 2 Lesson Objectives

- <u>Understand Character Relationships</u>: Students will analyze the relationships between John, Sally, Majasi, and Belinda.
- <u>Identify Cultural Conflicts</u>: Students will explore the cultural conflicts and personal differences highlighted in the scene.
- <u>Explore Themes</u>: Students will discuss themes of language, respect, and cultural identity.

- <u>Develop Critical Thinking</u>: Students will engage in discussions and activities to develop their critical thinking and analytical skills.

Activities

1. **Reading and Discussion**:
   - **Character Analysis**: Discuss the relationships between John, Sally, Majasi, and Belinda. What do their interactions reveal about their characters?

Discussion Questions

1. **Character Relationships**:
   - How does John's attempt to speak Shona to his grandfather reflect their relationship?
   - What does Sally's reaction to John speaking Shona reveal about her character and her relationship with Majasi?
2. **Themes**:
   - How does the scene explore the theme of language and cultural identity? Why is it significant that John tries to speak Shona to his grandfather?
   - What does Sally's disregard for traditional customs reveal about her views on cultural identity and respect?
3. **Conflict and Resolution**:
   - How does Belinda's respectful interaction with Majasi contrast with Sally's behavior, and what does this reveal about their characters?
4. **Personal Reflection**:
   - How do the characters' actions and decisions in this scene set the stage for future conflicts in the play?

NOTES:

Scene 3

SUMMARY: Sally and John return to the living room, where Majasi is listening to a mbira music radio program. John shares his sweets with his grandfather, showing their close relationship. Sally tells John to turn off the radio, pointedly expressing her dislike for mbira music. She instructs him to turn on the TV instead.

John turns on the TV and starts to go outside to play, but Sally orders him to come back and watch the Kiddie Program on TV, saying his white school friends might be on it. John protests, saying they aren't his friends and that only white children are allowed on the program. Sally insists that his friends are the white children on TV, not the neighborhood children he wants to play with, whom she considers dirty.

Benjani, the houseboy-servant, enters the scene, returning from the local store where he had gone to buy Sally's women's magazine. He informs Sally that the store hasn't received the latest edition of the magazine yet. Sally is upset and complains that everything arrives late to the African township. She then instructs Benjani to prepare dinner immediately because she and her husband Rwizi have ballroom dancing practice that night.

Rwizi arrives from work accompanied by his younger brother Andrew.

The love and respect that Majasi, Rwizi and Andrew show each other is self-evident in the way they greet each with their totem and the easy laughter which fills the living room. Sally is miffed at the arrival of Andrew who greets her in Shona.

Scene 3 Lesson Objectives

- <u>Understand Character Relationships</u>: Students will analyze the relationships between Sally, John, Majasi, Rwizi, Andrew, and Benjani.
- <u>Identify Cultural Conflicts</u>: Students will explore the cultural conflicts and generational differences highlighted in the scene.
- <u>Explore Themes</u>: Students will discuss themes of language, respect, cultural identity, and social expectations.

Activities

1. **Reading and Discussion**:
   - **Read the Scene Aloud**: Have students take turns reading the scene aloud in class.
   - **Character Analysis**: Discuss the relationships between Sally, John, Majasi, Rwizi, Andrew, and Benjani. What do their interactions reveal about their characters?

Discussion Questions

1. **Character Relationships**:
   - How does John's sharing of sweets with his grandfather reflect their relationship?
   - What does Sally's reaction to the mbira music reveal about her character and her relationship with Majasi?
2. **Themes**:

- How does the scene explore the theme of language and cultural identity? Why is it significant that John wants to play with neighborhood children rather than watch the Kiddie Program?
- What does Sally's disregard for traditional customs and her insistence on watching the Kiddie Program reveal about her views on cultural identity and social expectations?

3. **Conflict and Resolution**:
   - How does the arrival of Benjani and his interaction with Sally highlight the social and economic differences in the household?

4. **Personal Reflection**:
   - How do you think you would feel if you were in John's position? What would you do differently, if anything?
   - How do the characters' actions and decisions in this scene set the stage for future conflicts in the play?

NOTES

Scene 4   **SUMMARY:** Scenes 4 is the exposition of the play. In this scene, the main characters—Sally, Rwizi, Andrew, and Majasi—reveal their desires and the resulting obstacles and conflicts that arise there from. The action takes place in the privacy of Rwizi and Sally's bedroom. Sally is upset that Rwizi has brought his younger brother, Andrew, to their home. Rwizi explains that Andrew, who has finished Form 4, cannot return to their village home because it was burnt down by Rhodesia Army soldiers. Andrew is now relying on Rwizi for food and accommodation while he looks for work to support himself and their father, Majasi.

Sally believes her husband's family obligations are not her problem. She views Andrew and Majasi presence in their home as an obstacle to raising their son as an English-speaking, European-cultured person. Sally tells Rwizi that his father doesn't belong in their house and reminds him of their upcoming ballroom dancing competition and the after-party they are hosting in the house. She insists that Majasi doesn't fit the image she wants to present to their white, Indian, Coloured and wealthy African friends who are coming to Beatrice Cottages to her party. She threatens to leave with their son if Rwizi doesn't move his father out before the party. Rwizi pleads for more time, explaining that his father is mourning and needs time to recover. Sally suggests Rwizi finds a place where Majasi can receive medical care with other elderly African men.

This sets the stage for the events leading to Sally's party and Majasi's tragic demise.

Scene 4 Lesson Objectives

- <u>Understand Character Motivations</u>: Students will analyze the desires and motivations of the main characters (Sally, Rwizi, Andrew, and Majasi).
- <u>Identify Conflicts</u>: Students will identify the obstacles and conflicts that arise from the characters' desires.
- <u>Explore Themes</u>: Students will explore the themes of family obligations, cultural identity, and social expectations.

Activities

1. **Reading and Discussion**:
   - **Read Scene 4 Aloud**: Have students take turns reading the scene aloud in class.
   - **Character Analysis**: Discuss the motivations and desires of each character. What do they want, and what obstacles do they face?
2. **Group Activity**:
   - **Conflict Mapping**: In small groups, students will create a conflict map that outlines the main conflicts in the scene. They will identify the source of each conflict and how it affects the characters.
3. **Role-Playing**:
   - **Role-Playing Exercise**: Students will role-play the scene, focusing on the emotions and motivations of the characters. This will help them understand the

characters' perspectives and the dynamics of the scene.

Discussion Questions

1. **Character Motivations**:
   o What are Sally's main concerns and desires in this scene? How do they conflict with Rwizi's obligations to his family?
   o How does Andrew's presence in the house create tension between Sally and Rwizi?

2. **Themes**:
   o How does the scene explore the theme of cultural identity? How does Sally's desire to raise her son as an English-speaking, European-cultured person clash with Rwizi's family obligations?
   o What does this scene reveal about the social expectations and pressures faced by the characters?

3. **Conflict and Resolution**:
   o What are the main conflicts in this scene? How do the characters attempt to resolve these conflicts?
   o How does Sally's threat to leave with their son impact Rwizi's decisions and actions?

4. **Personal Reflection**:
   o How do you think you would feel if you were in Rwizi's position? What would you do differently, if anything?
   o How do the characters' actions and decisions in this scene set the stage for the events leading to Sally's party and Majasi's tragic demise?

OCT ONE   Lesson Plan – Scene 5

Scene 5

SUMMARY: Scene 5 highlights the social, economic, and political differences within the African majority population under the racist rule of the white minority government. Andrew gets to know his nephew John by asking about his school experience. John reveals he is bullied at his white school because he is black. When Andrew asks if John fights back, Sally admonishes Andrew, claiming he is encouraging violence. John questions why he can't fight back when called a "kaffir," and Sally's response is to ignore her son's situation at the white school and tells him that the white children are nice.

When dinner is served, Sally instructs Benjani to serve Majasi and Andrew on plates which he places on a tray at their feet while she and her husband and child eat at the table.

While they are having dinner Sally reminds Rwizi that they have ballroom dancing rehearsal to go to soon after dinner. Rwizi informs her that he cannot accompany her because he must attend a political meeting in the neighbourhood

Sally is shocked that Rwizi would rather attend a political meeting with "uneducated Africans" than go to their ballroom dancing dress rehearsal. She questions why he would associate with Africans who are demanding what they already have in Beatrice Cottages. Rwizi explains that his mother's death at the hands of Rhodesia Army soldiers made him reflect on the injustices faced by Africans. Sally dismisses these injustices and praises white rule, claiming it has benefited Africans who she believes are incapable of ruling themselves. Rwizi counters by mentioning independent African countries like Tanzania, Kenya, and Zambia. Sally remains unimpressed, insisting those countries would be better off under white rule.

Andrew respectfully reminds Sally that Africans were successful in ruling themselves before colonialism, citing the construction of Great Zimbabwe without white assistance. Sally dismisses him as a "communist puppy" and warns him to be cautious about discussing politics in front of John. Exasperated, Sally warns Rwizi against getting involved in the political movement, arguing that they don't need what the African nationalists want since they already have a nice house in Beatrice Cottages, a car, white friends, and good jobs. She insists they don't need majority rule.

Scene 5 Lesson Objectives

- <u>Understand Social and Political Context:</u> Students will analyze the social, economic, and political differences highlighted in the scene.
- <u>Character Analysis</u>: Students will explore the motivations and perspectives of all the characters (Sally, Rwizi, Andrew, John, and Benjani).
- <u>Identify Conflicts</u>: Students will identify the obstacles and conflicts that arise from the characters' desires and perspectives.

- Explore Themes: Students will discuss themes of racial oppression, cultural identity, and social expectations.

Discussion Questions

1. **Character Motivations**:
   - What are Sally's main concerns and desires in this scene? How do they conflict with Rwizi's political beliefs?
2. **Themes**:
   - How does the scene explore the theme of racial oppression? How do Sally's views on white rule contrast with Rwizi's and Andrew's perspectives?
   - What does this scene reveal about the social expectations and pressures faced by the characters?
3. **Conflict and Resolution**:
   - What are the main conflicts in this scene? How do the characters attempt to resolve these conflicts?
   - How does Sally's insistence on attending the ballroom dancing rehearsal impact Rwizi's decisions and actions?
4. **Personal Reflection**:
   - How do you think you would feel if you were in Rwizi's position? What would you do differently, if anything?
   - How do the characters' actions and decisions in this scene set the stage for future conflicts in the play?
   - What does Benjani's position and role say about this family?

Scene 6   SUMMARY: Scene 6 closes Act One. It begins in Sally and Rwizi's bedroom, where Sally prepares to leave for ballroom dancing dress rehearsals. She tries to persuade Rwizi to join her, but he flatters her by saying she's the best dancer and can teach him new dance patterns. After Sally leaves, Rwizi joins his father and brother in the living room and reveals that the clandestine political meeting he is attending is disguised as a "pungwe" all-night "bira," a Shona traditional religious rite with mbira players and drummers. This serves to cover up the political agenda from state security forces. When Andrew asks to join him, Majasi reminds Rwizi that Andrew is a mbira virtuoso. Rwizi agrees, saying Andrew's pan-Africanist views make him a natural fit for the meeting.

Scene 6 Lesson Objectives

- Understand Character Motivations: Students will analyze the desires and motivations of the main characters (Sally, Rwizi, Andrew, and Majasi).
- Identify Conflicts: Students will identify the obstacles and conflicts that arise from the characters' desires.
- Explore Themes: Students will explore the themes of cultural identity, political activism, and family obligations.

Discussion Questions

1. **Character Motivations**:

- What are Sally's main concerns and desires in this scene?

2. **Themes**:
   - How does the scene explore the theme of cultural identity? How does the use of the "pungwe" all-night "bira" serve as a cover for political activism?
   - What does this scene reveal about the social expectations and pressures faced by the characters?

3. **Conflict and Resolution**:
   - What are the main conflicts in this scene? How do the characters attempt to resolve these conflicts?
   - How does Sally's insistence on attending the ballroom dancing rehearsal impact Rwizi's decisions and actions?

4. **Personal Reflection**:
   - How do you think you would feel if you were in Andrew's position? What would you do differently, if anything?
   - How do the characters' actions and decisions in this scene set the stage for future conflicts in the play?

NOTES

OCT TWO   Lesson Plan (1 scene)

Act Two   SUMMARY: When Rwizi and Andrew arrive at the neighborhood house for the clandestine political meeting which was disguised as a bira, they are recognized by two lookouts and allowed to enter. The people in the house honour their African traditions by removing their shoes and wearing traditional attire. Rwizi, like the other men in the house, wears a fur hat. Inside, a bira fusion band plays a Chimurenga song. Andrew is drawn to Muchazo, a female mbira player leading the band. They exchange warm looks. After the song, the people shout slogans of liberation. Andrew picks up a mbira and joins the band, impressing everyone with his exceptional talent. Muchazo concedes the lead mbira solo to Andrew, and the band backs him up.

When Mr. Mlambo, the host and owner of the house, enters the living room, the band stops playing. Mr. Mlambo and Rwizi greet each other warmly. Rwizi introduces Andrew to Mr. Mlambo, who praises Andrew's mbira playing skills and requests the song "Nemhamusasa," which pays homage to the ancestors. Andrew and the band play the song, delighting everyone and prompting some people to dance.

The end of the song signals the start of the political discussion. Mr. Mlambo and Rwizi talk about the economy and the growing fear among the white community as the guerrilla war approaches their urban residential and commercial areas. Rwizi mentions the fear he senses at his workplace. He then gives Mr. Mlambo a financial donation for the guerrilla war effort to support the young fighters with food and provisions. Mr. Mlambo acknowledges the contribution and assures Rwizi that it is making a difference. Rwizi excuses himself, saying he must get up early for work, and leaves, allowing Andrew to stay and continue playing and getting acquainted with everyone.

Act 2 Lesson Objectives

- Understand Cultural and Political Context: Students will analyze the cultural and political significance of the clandestine meeting disguised as a bira.
- Character Analysis: Students will explore the motivations and perspectives of the main characters (Rwizi, Andrew, Mr. Mlambo, and Muchazo).
- Identify Conflicts: Students will identify the obstacles and conflicts that arise from the characters' desires and perspectives.
- Explore Themes: Students will discuss themes of cultural identity, political activism, and social expectations.

Discussion Questions

1. **Cultural Identity**: How do the characters in the scene navigate their cultural identities? How does the clandestine nature of the political meeting reflect their struggle for cultural preservation?

2. **Political Resistance**: What role does the liberation war play in shaping the characters' actions and relationships? How do the slogans of liberation and the financial donation reflect the characters' commitment to the political struggle?
3. **Role of Music**: How does music function as a cultural and political tool in this scene? In what ways does Andrew's mbira playing contribute to the theme of cultural resistance?
4. **Use of Space**: How is the use of domestic space (the neighborhood house) significant in this scene? What does the transformation of a private home into a space for political discourse and cultural expression reveal about the characters' lives?
5. **Symbolism**: What are the symbolic elements present in the scene, such as traditional attire, the mbira, and the song "Nemhamusasa"? How do these symbols enhance the thematic depth of the play?

1. **Character Relationships**:
   - How does Rwizi's greeting with the two lookouts at the entrance reveal about his relationship with the people in the political movement?
   - How does Andrew's interaction with Muchazo and the mbira band highlight his character development?
   - What does the mbira band openness to allow Andrew a total stranger to play with them reveal about the band and the nature of mbira music?
   - How does Mr. Mlambo's request for Andrew to play Nemhamusasa energize the meeting?
2. **Themes**:
   - How does the scene explore the issue of political identity?
   - What does the scene reveal about the commitment of the people in the meeting to the cause of freedom and independence?

- How does the mbira music serve as a symbol of cultural heritage and resistance?
- How does the scene inform on the use of space and location of the political meeting?
- What does the scene reveal about the social and political pressures faced by the characters, and how do these pressures influence their decisions?
-

3. **Conflict and Resolution**:
   - What are the main conflicts in this scene? How do the characters attempt to resolve these conflicts?
   - How do the characters' interactions set the stage for future conflicts and developments in the play?

4. **Personal Reflection**:
   - How do you think you would feel if you were in Mr. Mlambo's position? What would you do differently, if anything?
   - How do the characters' actions and decisions in this scene reflect their values and beliefs?

NOTES

OCT THREE Lesson Plan Scene 1   (3 months later)

Scene 1   SUMMARY: With mbira music playing on the radio in the house, Majasi and his grandson John are on the veranda, looking out to the street. John, playing with a toy car, asks his grandfather why he likes mbira music so much. Majasi explains it's traditional African music from "chinyakare," meaning a long time ago. He translates the word for John, who is excited to learn his grandfather speaks English. When John asks him why he acts as if he does not understand English, Majasi says he prefers Shona over English. When John mentions that his mother says Shona is for ignorant people and asks if Majasi is ignorant, Majasi responds in Shona, asking John's opinion. John reassures him, saying he's not ignorant and calls him his best friend, hugging him.

Majasi explains to John that he can speak English, but he prefers Shona, his own language. He encourages John to learn multiple languages, like English, Shona, and Ndebele. Majasi emphasizes that language is for communication, not for "kuvhayira" (bragging). When John asks what "kuvhayira" means, Majasi explains it as showing off and acting superior, which is not good. John repeats after his grandfather, agreeing that "kuvhayira" is not good.

Andrew arrives at the Choto House and joins his father and nephew on the veranda. To Andrew's delight, John demonstrates his knowledge of traditional Shona greetings by squatting and clapping his hands to greet Andrew.

When Benjani serves lunch to Majasi and Andrew where they sit, John complains about having to eat at the dining room table inside. With John back in the house, Majasi and Andrew discuss their lives. Andrew is concerned about Majasi's health, noting that he is wearing an overcoat despite the warm weather. Majasi dismisses it as a result of old age.

When Majasi asks about Andrew's job search, Andrew shares distressing news about police harassment due to his unemployment. He tells him he has been looking for work for 3 months with no prospects of ever getting one. He walks 5 miles daily to eat at Beatrice Cottages and lives in Matapi Hostels with 8 men in one room. He believes he won't find a job until his mother's spirit is at rest through traditional rites. Majasi encourages him to hang on, saying Rwizi will take care of them, and gives him a 2 dollar note. Andrew mentions the worsening economy and young people joining freedom fighters in Mozambique and Zambia. Majasi pleads with Andrew not to leave, as he is all Majasi has left.

After finishing lunch on the veranda, Andrew receives visitors: Chamu, the band leader, and Muchazo, his girlfriend. They stop by on their way to band rehearsal and are introduced to

Majasi, who is delighted to meet Andrew's friends with similar interests in mbira playing. The conversation is a mix of happy and sad moments as the three young mbira players share their struggles living in the township. Chamu, who completed Form 6, wanted to go to law school but is being called up for duty to fight the guerrillas. Muchazo, who completed Form 4, wants to become a nurse and has applied to a nursing school in the UK. Andrew, who also completed Form 4, cannot find a job to support his father. Muchazo gives Andrew a mbira instrument, paid for by the band members, inviting him to join the band. With no other employment prospects, Andrew joins the mbira band. Majasi encourages the young people, saying that the mbira instrument and music give them the courage to continue fighting the white minority regime until victory is won.

Majasi, Andrew, Chamu, and Muchazo are joined by an old man, Chaitezvi, Majasi's friend. Chaitezvi, tired and frustrated, explains that his 15-year-old grandson was arrested for being outside without his identity paper. Chaitezvi is alone at his son's house, as his son, a truck driver, is away moving white people fleeing the war in Rhodesia to South Africa. Chaitezvi's grandson, who looks older than 18, is detained at the local police station. Chaitezvi has not eaten because he doesn't know how to use the electric stove. Chamu and Muchazo assure Chaitezvi they will help get his grandson released and Muchazo will cook a meal for him and show him how to use the stove.

Scene 1 Lesson Objectives

- <u>Understand Character Relationships</u>: Students will analyze the relationships between Majasi, John, Andrew, Chamu, Muchazo and Chaitezvi.
- <u>Identify Cultural, Political and Social Issues</u>: Students will identify and explore all the cultural, social, and economic challenges faced by the characters.
- <u>Explore Themes</u>: Students will discuss themes of language, respect, cultural identity, political activism, family obligations, community and resilience.

Discussion Questions

5. **Character Relationships**:
    - How does John's attempt to speak Shona to his grandfather reflect their relationship?
    - What does Majasi's act of explaining a Shona word in English to John say about the nature of their relationship?
    - What does Andrew's arrival and interaction with John and Majasi reveal about their family dynamics?
    - How does Chamu and Muchazo's visit and their conversation with Majasi and Andrew highlight their shared struggles and aspirations?
    - How does Chaitezvi's situation reflect the challenges faced by the displaced elderly in the community?
    - What does the interaction between Chamu, Muchazo, and Chaitezvi reveal about their sense of community and support?
    -
6. **Themes**:

- How does the scene explore the theme of language and cultural identity? Why is it significant that Majasi wants John to learn multiple languages?
- What does the scene reveal about the social and economic pressures faced by the characters, and how do these pressures influence their decisions?
- How does the mbira music serve as a symbol of cultural heritage and resistance?
- How does the scene explore the theme of family support and community resilience? Why is it significant that Andrew, Chamu and Muchazo offer to help Chaitezvi?
- What does the scene reveal about the social and political pressures faced by the characters, and how do these pressures influence their decisions?

7. **Conflict and Resolution**:
   - What are the main conflicts in this scene? How do the characters attempt to resolve these conflicts?
   - How does Majasi's encouragement and support impact Andrew's decisions and actions?
   - How does the support from Chamu and Muchazo impact Chaitezvi's situation and outlook?
   - How do the characters' interactions set the stage for future conflicts and developments in the play?
8. **Personal Reflection**:
   - How do you think you would feel if you were in Andrew's position? What would you do differently, if anything?
   - How do you think you would feel if you were in Chaitezvi's position? What would you do differently, if anything?
   - How do the characters' actions and decisions in this scene reflect their values and beliefs?

NOTES

OCT THREE Lesson Plan (Scene 2)

Scene 2   SUMMARY: There is no one on the stage except for a cityscape painting which fills up the whole stage. On the painting are written the words, City of Salisbury, Revenue Department. The phone rings, and the call is answered by someone at the City of Salisbury, Revenue Department. The caller, Sally, asks to speak to her husband, Rwizi, in his office. Sally excitedly informs Rwizi that their names are listed as finalists for the ballroom dancing competition in the society section of the day's Herald newspaper. She then shares what she says is good news about finding a home for Rwizi's father through her professional connections. A fellow nurse matron has offered a bed for Rwizi's father in an old people's home affiliated with her hospital. When Rwizi learns the home is in Plumtree, 300 miles away, he protests, but Sally insists he can visit him there using their fast car, a Datsun 120Y. Rwizi is speechless. Sally ends the call, urging Rwizi to be grateful and decide quickly before the bed is given to someone else.

Scene 2 Lesson Objectives

- Understand Character Motivations: Students will analyze the motivations and desires of the two characters (Sally and Rwizi).
- Identify Conflicts: Students will identify the obstacles and conflicts that arise from the characters' desires.
- Explore Themes: Students will explore the themes of family obligations, cultural identity, and social expectations.

- Develop Critical Thinking: Students will engage in discussions and activities to develop their critical thinking and analytical skills.

Discussion Questions

1. **Character Motivations**:
   - What are Sally's main concerns and desires in this scene? How do they conflict with Rwizi's obligations to his family?
   - How does Rwizi's reaction to Sally's solution for his father reveal his values and priorities?

2. **Themes**:
   - How does the scene explore the theme of family obligations? How does Sally's solution for Rwizi's father reflect her views on family and responsibility?
   - What does this scene reveal about the social expectations and pressures faced by the characters?

3. **Conflict and Resolution**:
   - What are the main conflicts in this scene? How do the characters attempt to resolve these conflicts?
   - How does Sally's insistence on placing Rwizi's father in a home far away impact their relationship?

4. **Personal Reflection**:
   - How do you think you would feel if you were in Rwizi's position? What would you do differently, if anything?
   - How do the characters' actions and decisions in this scene set the stage for future conflicts in the play?

NOTES

OCT FOUR   Lesson Plan (1 scene)

Act 4   SUMMARY: On a late Saturday afternoon, Rwizi and Sally are entertaining Belinda and her husband, Sam, at Choto House. Majasi and John are also present, with John drawing a picture for his grandfather. The atmosphere is casual as Rwizi, Sally, and Belinda enjoy cocktails. Sam leaves to go and attend to his retail shop which is struggling due to the worsening economy. Belinda brings presents for Majasi and John, including sweets for John, biscuits for Majasi, and a hat for Majasi, which moves him visibly.

Belinda notices that Majasi seems unwell and expresses her concern to Sally, who dismisses it as mild fatigue. Belinda checks Majasi's temperature and suggests he might be constipated due to dehydration. Rwizi and John help Majasi to his bedroom to rest, leaving Sally and Belinda alone.

Belinda compliments Sally on taking care of Majasi. Belinda opines that having Majasi around is beneficial for John's upbringing, teaching him "ubuntu" (African humanity) but Sally dismisses Belinda's opinion. Sally tells Belinda that John doesn't need "ubuntu" as he attends an expensive white school where he will get all the European culture, she wants him to have. Sally then changes the subject to their ballroom dancing competition, which Belinda finds uninteresting. Sally boasts about their potential win, while Belinda retorts that she doesn't care about ballroom dancing and isn't a "high class native" like Sally. Sally responds by

55

emphasizing their social status and newspaper recognition.

Act 4 Lesson Objectives

- <u>Understand Character Relationships</u>: Students will analyze the relationships between Rwizi, Sally, Belinda, Sam, Majasi, and John.
- <u>Identify Social and Cultural Issues</u>: Students will explore the social and cultural challenges faced by the characters.
- <u>Explore Themes</u>: Students will discuss themes of family support, cultural identity, social status, and generational differences.
- <u>Develop Critical Thinking</u>: Students will engage in discussions and activities to develop their critical thinking and analytical skills.

Activities

1. **Reading and Discussion**:
   - **Read the Scene Aloud**: Have students take turns reading the scene aloud in class.
   - **Character Analysis**: Discuss the motivations and perspectives of each character especially the differences between Belinda and Sally in regards to "ubuntu".

Discussion Questions

1. **Character Relationships**:
   - How does the interaction between Sally and Belinda reveal their differing views on family and cultural identity?
   - What does Majasi's reaction to the presents from Belinda reveal about his character and his relationship with her?

2. **Themes**:
    - How does the scene explore the theme of cultural identity? How do Sally and Belinda's views on raising John differ?
    - What does the scene reveal about the social and economic pressures faced by the characters, and how do these pressures influence their decisions?
    - What does Sam's decision to forgo the cocktails to go to attend to his struggling retail business say about the economy and its impact on business owners?
3. **Conflict and Resolution**:
    - What are the main conflicts in this scene? How do the characters attempt to resolve these conflicts?
    - How does the conversation between Sally and Belinda highlight the cultural differences in their perspectives?
4. **Personal Reflection**:
    - How do you think you would feel if you were in Belinda's position? What would you do differently, if anything?
    - How do the characters' actions and decisions in this scene reflect their values and beliefs?

NOTES

OCT FIVE   Lesson Plan (1 scene)

Act 5

SUMMARY: In Act 5, Andrew arrives at Mlambo house for band practice, which will lead into a bira that night. This is his first full band rehearsal due to the distance he has to walk from Matapi Hostels, police patrols, and job hunting. He finds only Chamu and Muchazo present, playing a slow, sad mbira song. Andrew joins them, and they play two songs before he takes a break to rest for the long night ahead.

Chamu tells Andrew that Muchazo may have solved his accommodation problems. Muchazo tells Andrew he can have a job working for her rich uncle. She says he can get the job working as a tutor for a Form 2 child and a garden boy for her wealthy uncle in Marimba Park, an exclusive suburb for wealthy Africans in Salisbury. The job comes with a salary and a two-bedroom boy's kaya in the back of the house. Andrew is excited and hugs Muchazo, thanking her for the opportunity to take care of his father with dignity.

Chamu then reveals that the other four band members have left the country overnight to join the freedom fighters in Zambia and Mozambique. Andrew is disappointed but understands their decision, expressing his own desire to leave to go and fight the racist minority white government. Chamu quotes Franz Fanon, saying, "every generation must find its purpose, and fulfill or betray it." Chamu says he has found his own purpose in the mbira band and believes mbira music will lead their people to victory.

Muchazo then hands Andrew a letter of admission she received from a nursing school in the UK, along with a full scholarship from the British Council. After reading the letter, Andrew is visibly dejected.

Muchazo comforts Andrew, asking why he is sad when he now has a job and a home for his father. Andrew expresses his disappointment, saying he thought his luck had changed now that he is a member of a band, as well as having Muchazo, and the job. Muchazo reassures him that she will not forget him when she goes to the UK and they will write to each other via airmail. Chamu adds that mbira music doesn't need a large band, as it belongs to the ancestors who will choose new band members. He encourages Andrew to cheer up and let Muchazo go, reminding him that she loves him and always will.

Act 5 Lesson Objectives

- Understand Character Relationships: Students will analyze the relationships between Andrew, Chamu, and Muchazo.
- Identify Social and Political Issues: Students will explore the social and political challenges faced by the characters.
- Explore Themes: Students will discuss themes of cultural identity, political activism, and personal aspirations.

Activities

Discussion Questions

1. **Character Relationships**:
   - How does Andrew's interaction with Chamu and Muchazo reflect their friendship and shared struggles?
   - What does Muchazo's offer of a job and accommodation reveal about her character and her relationship with Andrew?

2. **Themes**:
   - How does the scene explore the theme of cultural identity? How do the characters' interests in mbira music and traditional rites reflect their cultural heritage?
   - What does the scene reveal about the social and political pressures faced by the characters, and how do these pressures influence their decisions?
   - What does the scene reveal about the young people who left their friends and family to go and join the freedom fighters in Mozambique and Zambia?

3. **Conflict and Resolution**:
   - What are the main conflicts in this scene? How do the characters attempt to resolve these conflicts?
   - How does Chamu's and Muchazo's support impact Andrew's decisions and actions?
   -

4. **Personal Reflection**:
   - How do you think you would feel if you were in Andrew's position? What would you do differently, if anything?
   - How do the characters' actions and decisions in this scene reflect their values and beliefs?

NOTES:

ACT SIX   Lesson Plan (1 scene)

Act 6

SUMMARY: It is in the evening at Choto house. Rwizi and Sally are alone in the living room, rehearsing for the upcoming ballroom dancing competition in their practice costumes. They are dancing to Beethoven's Waltz in E Flat Major, laughing and having a great time. When the record ends, Rwizi admits he is tired, but Sally insists they continue practicing. She excuses herself to go to the bathroom while Rwizi refreshes their cocktail glasses.

While Sally is in the bathroom, there is a knock at the door. Rwizi answers and finds an old woman with a bundle, asking if this is the house where a nurse from Mutoko lives. Assuming she is looking for Sally, Rwizi lets her in. The old woman enters and sits by the door with her bundle.

Sally comes out of the bathroom and sees the old woman, assuming she is one of Rwizi's relatives. She calls Rwizi to the bedroom, where she learns the woman claims to be her relative. Mystified, Sally asks the woman to explain how she is related to her. The woman tells a long, sad story about government soldiers burning down her village with napalm bombs and killing suspected anti-government sympathizers. Sally impatiently acknowledges the woman's loss but insists on knowing how she is related to her. Finally, the woman tentatively reveals she is Sally's aunt. Sally responds that the woman must be mistaken, as she believes she has no African relatives, only a white missionary doctor in Mutoko. Sally presses the woman to explain how she could be her aunt.

When the woman reveals she is Sally's mother's older sister, Sally erupts, demanding to know how she found her and where she was when Sally's mother was banished after being raped by her father, making the woman Sally's stepsister, not aunt. The woman pleads ignorance of her father's deed and asks for a place to stay, as she is now homeless. Sally orders her out and threatens her with a broom. Rwizi restrains Sally, allowing the woman to escape. After the woman leaves, Sally reminds Rwizi that he must find accommodation for his father before the regional ballroom dancing competition finals in less than three weeks.

Act 6 Lesson Plan Objectives

- <u>Understand Character Relationships</u>: Students will analyze the relationships between Rwizi, Sally, and the old woman.
- <u>Identify Social and Cultural Issues</u>: Students will explore the social and cultural challenges faced by the characters.
- <u>Explore Themes</u>: Students will discuss themes of family, cultural identity, and social expectations.

Activities

Discussion Questions

1. **Character Relationships**:
   o How does the interaction between Sally and the old woman reveal their differing views on family and cultural identity?

- What does Rwizi's reaction to the old woman's arrival reveal about his character and his relationship with Sally?

2. **Themes**:
   - How does the scene explore the theme of family obligations? How do Sally and Rwizi's responses to the old woman reflect their views on family and responsibility?
   - What does the scene reveal about the social expectations and pressures faced by the characters?

3. **Conflict and Resolution**:
   - What are the main conflicts in this scene? How do the characters attempt to resolve these conflicts?
   - How does the old woman's story impact Sally and Rwizi's relationship and their decisions?

4. **Personal Reflection**:
   - How do you think you would feel if you were in the old woman's position? What would you do differently, if anything?
   - How do you think you would feel if you were in Sally's position? What would you do differently, if anything?
   - How do the characters' actions and decisions in this scene reflect their values and beliefs?

NOTES:

ACT SEVEN Lesson Plan (1 scene)

| **Act 7** | SUMMARY: The action is set in Rwizi's office during the day. Andrew, who now has a job, has visited Beatrice Cottages and learned from the houseboy Benjani that Rwizi took Majasi home. Confused, Andrew has come to Rwizi's office to find out where "home" is, as their village in |

Mhondoro was burned down by Rhodesian soldiers after their mother was killed.

When Andrew greets Rwizi, Rwizi appears nervous and tries to make small talk, asking where Andrew has been since he hasn't seen him at the house for two weeks. Andrew explains that he stopped coming because Benjani told him Sally didn't want him there anymore. Rwizi insists it's a misunderstanding, saying Sally only mentioned that Andrew was dirtying the house when playing with John.

Andrew dismisses the explanation, stating that he only wants to know where their father is. Rwizi avoids answering directly, instead talking about the pressures Sally and he face at their jobs. Frustrated, Andrew asks what that has to do with their father's whereabouts. Rwizi suggests that if they had relatives, their father would live with them. Andrew, flabbergasted, points out that they are closest of relatives, being blood relatives, and it doesn't get any closer than that.

Rwizi suggests that if Andrew had a job, things might be different. Andrew interrupts, stating that he does have a job and had planned to tell their father so he could move in with him. Andrew's boss is a traditional African who understands the plight of Africans. Rwizi praises Andrew for securing a job in a tough market, but Andrew dismisses the praise, emphasizing that he is just a garden boy working for a sympathetic African tycoon. He demands to know where their father is.

Rwizi reluctantly reveals that he placed their father in an old people's home in Plumtree, 300 miles away from Salisbury. Andrew is furious and berates Rwizi for being heartless. When Rwizi asks him to lower his voice, Andrew raises it even louder, wanting everyone to know what kind of man Rwizi is. Eventually, Andrew calms down and asks for the exact location in Plumtree. Rwizi provides directions and bus fare, which Andrew reluctantly accepts because he has no money. However, Andrew declares that they are no longer brothers and leaves.

Lesson Plan Objectives for Act 7

- <u>Understand Character Relationships</u>: Students will analyze the relationship between Andrew and Rwizi.
- <u>Identify Social and Cultural Issues</u>: Students will explore the social and cultural challenges faced by the characters.
- <u>Explore Themes</u>: Students will discuss themes of family obligations, cultural identity, and social expectations.

Activities

1. **Role-Playing**:
   - **Role-Playing Exercise**: Students will role-play the scene, focusing on the emotions and motivations of the characters. This will help them understand the characters' perspectives and the dynamics of the scene.

Discussion Questions

1. **Character Relationships**:

- How does Andrew's interaction with Rwizi reveal their differing views on family and responsibility?
- What does Rwizi's nervousness and avoidance of direct answers indicate about his character and his relationship with Andrew?

2. **Themes**:
   - How does the scene explore the theme of family obligations? How do Andrew and Rwizi's responses to their father's situation reflect their views on family and responsibility?
   - What does the scene reveal about the social and economic pressures faced by the characters, and how do these pressures influence their decisions?

3. **Conflict and Resolution**:
   - What are the main conflicts in this scene? How do the characters attempt to resolve these conflicts?
   - How does Andrew's reaction to Rwizi's decision impact their relationship and the dynamics of the scene?

4. **Personal Reflection**:
   - How do you think you would feel if you were in Andrew's position? What would you do differently, if anything?
   - How do the characters' actions and decisions in this scene reflect their values and beliefs?

NOTES

ACT EIGHT   Lesson Plan (1 scene)

Act 8

SUMMARY: Andrew has traveled to Plumtree to bring his father back to live with him in Marimba Park. He is sitting on a tree stump at the bus stop, near a sign pointing to the *Plumtree Shelter for the Old*. Andrew, with a brown paper bag containing Majasi's hat and other belongings, is crying and playing his mbira. Two men in military fatigues approach him and introduce themselves as guerrilla fighters who control the area.

Andrew reveals that his father, Majasi, has died. The men pay their respects and condolences, telling Andrew that his father's loss is their loss too. Andrew is delighted to meet them and sees their appearance as a sign from the ancestors and his dead father, indicating that he should join the guerrillas. The men welcome him to the fight for liberation and ask about his plans. Andrew explains that he had intended to go back to Salisbury to inform his brother, Rwizi, that he (Rwizi) had accomplished his goal of getting rid of their father. However, he has changed his mind and has now decided to bury his father in Plumtree and join the guerrillas, because he believes Rwizi doesn't care.

The men are taken aback by Andrew's bitterness towards his brother. They offer to help bury Majasi. They offer to make the burial casket, and take Andrew to their training camp. Andrew is surprised and grateful for their assistance. The guerrillas persuade Andrew to return to Salisbury to inform his brother about their father's death and deliver a package for them. Andrew agrees, and one of the men gives him a brown bag, revealing it contains a bomb. Andrew, undeterred, agrees to carry the brown paper bag along with his own on the bus to Salisbury.

Lesson Plan Objectives for Act 8

- <u>Understand Character Relationships</u>: Students will analyze the relationships between Andrew, the guerrilla fighters, and his brother Rwizi.
- <u>Identify Social and Political Issues</u>: Students will explore the social and political challenges faced by the characters.
- <u>Explore Themes</u>: Students will discuss themes of family obligations, political activism, and personal sacrifice.

Activities

1. **Reading and Discussion**:
   - **Read the Scene Aloud**: Have students take turns reading the scene aloud in class.
   - **Character Analysis**: Discuss the motivations and perspectives of each character. What do they want, and what obstacles do they face?

Discussion Questions

1. **Character Relationships**:
   - How does Andrew's interaction with the guerrilla fighters reveal his feelings towards his brother Rwizi?
   - What does the guerrilla fighters' offer to help bury Majasi and take Andrew to their training camp reveal about their values and beliefs?
2. **Themes**:

- How does the scene explore the theme of family obligations? How do Andrew's actions reflect his sense of duty towards his father?
- What does the scene reveal about the social and political pressures faced by the characters, and how do these pressures influence their decisions?

3. **Conflict and Resolution**:
   - What are the main conflicts in this scene? How do the characters attempt to resolve these conflicts?
   - How does Andrew's decision to join the guerrillas and deliver the package impact his relationship with his brother and his own sense of identity?

4. **Personal Reflection**:
   - How do you think you would feel if you were in Andrew's position? What would you do differently, if anything?
   - How do you think you would feel if you were in the guerrilla fighters' position? What would you do differently, if anything?
   - How do the characters' actions and decisions in this scene reflect their values and beliefs?

NOTES

ACT NINE   Lesson Plan (1 scene)

Act 9   SUMMARY: It is nighttime in Beatrice Cottages at Choto House. Sally and Rwizi have won the ballroom dancing contest. The music is lively and there is celebration in the air. Sally's party is on. The guests at the party are white, Indian, Colored and wealthy Africans. All dressed in gowns and tuxedoes. These are the members of the various racially segregated Rhodesia European Classical Music Ballroom Dancing Clubs who have come together to Choto House to party. The highlight of the party will be the trophy presentation ceremony.

As the Herald newspaper photographer clicks away, the champagne is flowing freely. John, who has been allowed to stay up past his normal bedtime is dressed in a tuxedo enjoying himself with the adults. Benjani dressed in his houseboy-servant uniform is walking around picking up empty glasses and bottles. Among the guests also dressed up and having a good time are Belinda and Sam.

The Master of Ceremony, Mr. Goto, holding the gold plated champion's trophy in his hand, calls for silence among the party guests to give the guest of honour, Mr. Simon McIntyre, a chance to propose a toast. Mr. McIntyre, who is a white man, makes his toast saying ladies and gentlemen, it is an honor to celebrate our 1977 Rhodesia Ballroom Dancing Association champions, Sally and Rwizi Choto. He says the event exemplifies the friendship across colour lines in Rhodesia and counters accusations of oppression of Africans in Rhodesia by white people. He says Sally and Rwizi represent African prosperity, showing that hard work and education provide equal opportunities for all races in Rhodesia...this room is filled with success. The guests cheer him on.

McIntyre continues his toast saying "Before I present the trophy and toast our champions, Rwizi and Sally, I want to make a statement. I don't want to make this a political toast, but it hurts so much when these Zapu and Zanu communists in Maputo and Lusaka lie and accuse white people in Rhodesia of being racists. Our Rhodesia Ballroom Dancing Association has different ballroom dancing clubs under its umbrella, each race with its own club and its own residential area, but I can come here, to an African house to a party and so can Sally and Rwizi come to mine. Our ballroom dancing association is a good example of racial separation in harmony in Rhodesia."

While McIntyre is making his speech, Andrew arrives at the house with his two brown paper bags and stands on the veranda. John sees him and excitedly comes to tell him to join the party. Andrew asks John to go back and get his father, Rwizi, who is tipsy from champagne. Rwizi is happy to see Andrew and assumes he has brought their father back. However, Andrew informs him that their father is dead. Devastated, Rwizi collapses and begins to cry, with John following suit.

Sally, also tipsy, standing with her guests waiting to receive her trophy, sees Andrew through the open door standing in the veranda. She leaves the party to confront Andrew for coming to the house in his unwashed state. Andrew who has just travelled 600 miles round trip explains he came to inform Rwizi about their father's death. Sally accuses him of being spiteful and demands to know why he (Andrew) could not find some other time to tell Rwizi about it at his office. Rwizi tells Sally to leave Andrew alone; crying telling her that his father is dead. Rwizi is shocked when Sally tells him that she already knew that his father was dead. Rwizi demands to know why she had not told him about his father's death. Sally ignores Rwizi. She is focused on throwing Andrew out of her house. Sally lunges at Andrew who is holding the two brown paper bags. As he loses his footing, the brown bag with Majasi's hat is caught in Sally's pointing finger and tears scattering the hat and the rest of its contents on the ground. Andrew falls on his back gingerly holding the bag with bomb on his chest.

Rwizi threatens Sally and demands that she goes back into the house and leave them alone to mourn their father. When Sally asks what the guests will say if Rwizi doesn't come back to the party. He tells her, he does not care. He has been a fool. He is leaving with his son and brother to go and bury his father. When John goes into the house to get his father's wallet and car keys, Belinda follows John out of the house and finds the hat she gave to Majasi lying on the ground. When she asks why the hat is on the ground, Rwizi tells her his father is dead. Belinda starts crying and asks where Majasi is. Rwizi tells her Plumtree. When Belinda asks why Majasi died in Plumtree when she had assumed all along that he was sleeping in the bedroom while the party was going on. Rwizi tells her to ask her friend, Sally, why his father is dead in Plumtree.

Act 9 Lesson Plan Objectives

- <u>Understand Character Relationships</u>: Students will analyze the relationships between Sally, Rwizi, Andrew and the party guests.
- <u>Identify Social and Cultural Issues</u>: Students will explore the social and cultural dynamics of the scene.
- <u>Explore Themes</u>: Students will discuss themes of racial harmony, social status, and cultural identity.

Activities to Develop Critical Thinking:
Students will engage in discussions and activities to develop their critical thinking and analytical skills.

1. **Reading and Discussion**:
   - **Read the Scene Aloud**: Have students take turns reading the scene aloud in class.
   - **Character Analysis**: Discuss the motivations and perspectives of each character. What do they want, and what obstacles do they face?
2. **Group Activity**:
   - **Conflict Mapping**: In small groups, students will create a conflict map that outlines the main conflicts in the scene. They will identify the source of each conflict and how it affects the characters.
3. **Role-Playing**:

- o **Role-Playing Exercise**: Students will role-play the scene, focusing on the emotions and motivations of the characters. This will help them understand the characters' perspectives and the dynamics of the scene.

Discussion Questions

1. **Character Relationships**:
   - o How do Sally and Rwizi's interactions with the party guests reveal their social status and cultural identity?
   - o What does the presence of diverse guests at the party indicate about the social dynamics in Rhodesia?
   - o How does Andrew's interaction with Rwizi and Sally reveal their differing views on family and responsibility?
   - o What does Rwizi's reaction to the news of his father's death reveal about his character and his relationship with Andrew?

2. **Themes**:
   - o How does the scene explore the theme of racial harmony? How do the interactions between the guests reflect this theme?
   - o What does the scene reveal about the social and cultural pressures faced by the characters, and how do these pressures influence their decisions?
   - o How does the scene explore the theme of family obligations? How do Andrew and Rwizi's responses to their father's death reflect their views on family and responsibility?
   - o

3. **Conflict and Resolution**:
   - o What are the main conflicts in this scene? How do the characters attempt to resolve these conflicts?
   - o How does Mr. McIntyre's toast impact the atmosphere of the party and the relationships between the characters?

- How does Sally's reaction to Andrew's arrival impact the atmosphere of the party and the relationships between the characters?

4. **Personal Reflection**:
   - How do you think you would feel if you were in Sally or Rwizi's position? What would you do differently, if anything?
   - How do you think you would feel if you were in Andrew's position? What would you do differently, if anything?
   - How do the characters' actions and decisions in this scene reflect their values and beliefs?

NOTES

EPILOGUE   Lesson Plan (Act 9, scene 2)

Scene 2   SUMMARY: When the lights come on, we are in Choto's living room. The guests have left. Belinda still holding Majasi's hat, is standing being consoled by Sam.
Sally is sitting in a chair alone, holding the ballroom champion trophy in her lap.

Sam asks what is happening as Belinda cries and Sally remains silent. Sally, talking to herself, blames Andrew for ruining the party. Sam asks Belinda what happened, and she says Rwizi told her to ask Sally why his father was in Plumtree. Sally continues to lament the ruined party. Belinda tells them that she told the guests that Rwizi's father, who she thought was sleeping, was dead and the Rwizi was not coming back. That is why the guests left.

Sally insists that the guests had no reason to leave because Rwizi's father died in Plumtree, not at the house. Sam is confused and asks why Majasi was in Plumtree. Sally explains she found him a home there, recommended by her friend. She did not want Majasi in her house because of his influence on John. Sam is shocked and questions why Rwizi agreed. Sally says Majasi didn't belong in their European cultured home and was better off with other Shona-speaking Africans. She admits she didn't tell Rwizi about his father's death, fearing he would leave her. Belinda is astonished that Sally had known that Majasi had been dead for two days and had not told Rwizi

Sally explains that she intended to inform Rwizi about his father's death after the party, ensuring their guests had a good time and their pictures appeared in the newspaper. Sally defends her decision by arguing that it wouldn't have made a difference and that Rwizi would have abandoned their championship efforts. Belinda calls Sally mad for prioritizing the party over informing Rwizi about his father's death, but Sally insists she was not responsible for Majasi's death.

Realizing she may have lost her family as Rwizi left with their son, Sally feels distraught and helpless. Sam advises her to think about how to make things right, but Sally is unsure of what to do. Out of loyalty to her friend, Belinda advises Sally to discard the ballroom dancing trophy and apologize to Rwizi before he buries his father and their marriage. Sam persuades Belinda take Sally with them to drive to Plumtree to help Rwizi bury his father. Despite her frustration with Sally's obsession with European culture, Belinda agrees to help.

Belinda instructs Sally to change into appropriate funeral attire, including a headscarf (dhoek) and a Zambia wraparound cloth. Belinda and Sam plan to honor Sekuru Majasi at the funeral, and Sally is relieved and grateful to join them.

Lesson Plan Objectives for Epilogue (scene 2)

- **Understand Character Relationships**: Students will analyze the relationships between Sally, Rwizi, Belinda, and Sam.
- **Identify Social and Cultural Issues**: Students will explore the social and cultural dynamics of the scene.
- **Explore Themes**: Students will discuss themes of family obligations, social status, and cultural identity.
- **Develop Critical Thinking**: Students will engage in discussions and activities to develop their critical thinking and analytical skills.

Activities

1. **Reading and Discussion**:
   - o **Read the Scene Aloud**: Have students take turns reading the scene aloud in class.
   - o **Character Analysis**: Discuss the motivations and perspectives of each character. What do they want, and what obstacles do they face?

Discussion Questions

1. **Character Relationships**:
   - o How does Sally's interaction with Belinda and Sam reveal her priorities and values?
   - o What does Belinda's reaction to Sally's actions indicate about her character and her relationship with Sally?
2. **Themes**:
   - o How does the scene explore the theme of family obligations? How do Sally's actions reflect her sense of duty towards her family?
   - o What does the scene reveal about the social and cultural pressures faced by the characters, and how do these pressures influence their decisions?
3. **Conflict and Resolution**:
   - o What are the main conflicts in this scene? How do the characters attempt to resolve these conflicts?
   - o How does Sally's decision to prioritize the party over informing Rwizi about his father's death impact her relationships with the other characters?
4. **Personal Reflection**:
   - o How do you think you would feel if you were in Sally's position? What would you do differently, if anything?
   - o How do you think you would feel if you were in Belinda's position? What would you do differently, if anything?
   - o How do the characters' actions and decisions in this scene reflect their values and beliefs?

Chapter 5

A. CHARACTER ANALYSIS

1.   MAJASI

Resilience and Strength

Majasi is a character who embodies resilience, tradition, and the struggles of the older generation in adapting to a changing socio-political landscape. Despite enduring significant trauma, including the loss of his wife and the destruction of his village, Majasi remains determined to support his family, showcasing his resilience and strength.

Traditional Values

As a custodian of traditional Shona values, Majasi holds onto cultural heritage, emphasizing family, community, and ancestral customs. He relies on his son Rwizi for support, highlighting the challenges faced by the older generation in a rapidly changing society. The contrast between his traditional village life and the isolating urban environment underscores his vulnerability and dependence.

Vulnerability and Dependence

Majasi's presence in Rwizi's home creates cultural tension with Sally, who aspires to a European lifestyle, representing the broader conflict between tradition and modernity. His appreciation for mbira music symbolizes his connection to African traditions, contrasting with Sally's preference for European classical music.

Symbol of Cultural Conflict

Through Majasi, the play explores themes of family obligations, cultural identity, and the tension between preserving cultural heritage and adapting to modern influences. His character underscores the importance of cultural heritage and the difficulties faced by those striving to preserve it amidst rapid change.

Conclusion

Majasi represents the older generation's struggles in adapting to a changing world, showcasing resilience and adherence to traditional values. His challenges in the city highlight the complexities of cultural assimilation and the impact of socio-political changes on personal lives. Through Majasi, the play explores family obligations, cultural identity, and the tension between tradition and modernity, emphasizing the importance of cultural heritage and the difficulties in preserving it amidst rapid change.

2.   RWIZI

Rwizi is deeply committed to his family, feeling a strong sense of duty to care for both his nuclear family and his extended family. He cares for his elderly father, Majasi, and his younger brother, Andrew, as per Shona tradition. At the same time, he is dedicated to his wife, Sally, and their son, John. Balancing these conflicting demands creates significant tension in his life.

Cultural Conflict

Rwizi embodies the cultural conflict experienced by many Africans during this period. He respects and values his traditional Shona heritage but is also influenced by the modern, European lifestyle that Sally aspires to. He often finds himself as a mediator, trying to reconcile the cultural differences between his father and brother, who represent traditional values, and his wife, who rejects those traditions in favor of European culture.

Professional Success

Rwizi has achieved professional success as a deputy manager in the City of Salisbury's Revenue Services Department. His education and hard work have secured him a coveted position, providing financial stability for his family. He is grateful to his father for the sacrifices made to ensure his education and success, which reinforces his sense of obligation to care for his father in his old age.

Internal Struggle

Rwizi's internal struggle is characterized by his conflicting loyalties to his extended family and his nuclear family. He is torn between fulfilling his traditional responsibilities and supporting his wife's aspirations for a European lifestyle. His clandestine support for the liberation movements adds another layer to his internal conflict, as he navigates the dangers of political involvement while maintaining appearances for the safety of his family.

Compassion and Empathy

Rwizi demonstrates compassion and empathy towards his father and brother, understanding their plight and the challenges they face. He tries to support them while also respecting Sally's wishes. Despite the tension and conflict, Rwizi remains patient and strives to find a balance that will satisfy both his wife and his extended family.

In summary, Rwizi's character is marked by his deep commitment to family, cultural conflict, professional success, internal struggle, and compassion. He navigates the complexities of balancing traditional responsibilities with modern aspirations, making him a multifaceted and relatable character. Through Rwizi, the play explores themes of family obligations, cultural identity, and the tension between tradition and modernity

3.   SALLY

Sally is assertive and unafraid to voice her opinions and demands. Regardless of the consequences, she sets clear ultimatums and expects action rather than passive consideration. Her approach to life involves prioritizing her goals and taking practical steps to achieve them, such as insisting on raising her son with European values and enrolling him in an exclusive school.

Cultural Conflict
Sally rejects African traditions and aspires to a European nuclear family lifestyle. She insists on speaking only English in the house and raising her son, John, to be a European-cultured person. Her dedication to ballroom dancing and practicing in full costume reflects her commitment to her cause in pursuit of the European culture which is symbolized by ballroom dancing in the play. This desire to assimilate into European culture stems from her deep-seated resentment towards her African heritage.

Traumatic Past
Sally's traumatic childhood, marked by rejection and hardship, has left her with a deep-seated resentment towards her African heritage. Her mother was raped by her own father, and Sally's mother was blamed and ostracized by their village. This trauma has shaped Sally's rejection of African traditions and her desire to build a new identity. As a result, she is emotionally guarded and lacks empathy, prioritizing her own desires over the needs of her family and being unwilling to accommodate her in-laws.

Social Aspirations
Sally is concerned with maintaining a certain social status and image. Hosting the ballroom dancing club party reflects her desire to be seen as part of the upper middle class. Her obsession with European culture and disdain for African traditions create significant tension in her relationships, particularly with her husband, Rwizi. She is determined to raise her son with European values, even if it means alienating her in-laws.

Internal Conflict
Sally's internal conflict is evident in her struggle to reconcile her African heritage with her adopted European values. This cultural conflict leads to tension in her relationships and influences her actions and attitudes. Despite her harsh exterior, Sally's actions are

driven by a fear of losing the life she has worked hard to build. She is determined to protect her social status and the European identity she has created for herself and her family.

In summary, Sally is a complex character shaped by her traumatic past and her desire to build a new identity. Her assertiveness, pragmatism, and dedication to European values create significant tension in her relationships and highlight the cultural conflict within the narrative. Through Sally, the play explores themes of identity, cultural assimilation, and the struggle to reconcile conflicting values.

4.   ANDREW

Andrew serves as a bridge between the generations in the story. He stands at the intersection of his father Majasi's generation, his brother Rwizi's generation, his own generation, and his nephew John's generation. Andrew is the central character around whom the other characters define themselves, either as protagonists or antagonists.

Through his life the story explores the misdirection of government policies of that era, living and interacting with people who benefited from the status quo, like his sister-in-law, Sally, and those who suffered under it, like his father Majasi, Chaitezvi, and the mbira band members. Andrew also represents the uncertain future of his nephew John, who, despite his parents' financial means, faces bullying and racial marginalization at school.

Andrew's character highlights the contrast between those who gained from the oppressive system and those who were its victims, as well as the challenges faced by the younger generation. He is a testament to the complexities and struggles of navigating a society marked by deep-seated inequalities and cultural conflicts

Andrew is a multifaceted character, embodying resilience, cultural pride, and determination. His intelligence, musical talent, and connection to traditional values make him a symbol of hope. Through Andrew, the play explores themes of cultural identity, family dynamics, and the impact of war, offering a poignant commentary on the era. His strength, resilience, and commitment to cultural heritage and political beliefs underscore his role as a character willing to stand up against socio-political injustices, showcasing his integrity and determination. Additionally, his decision to stay and support his father, rather than joining the freedom fighters, highlights his sense of duty and familial responsibility amidst the chaos of war.

Cultural Connection

Andrew's proficiency with the mbira, highlights his deep connection to his cultural roots. His participation in mbira gatherings and leadership in songs underscore his commitment to preserving traditional values amidst changing times.

Impact of War

The socio-political climate and war have profoundly affected Andrew's life, displacing him from his home and leaving his future uncertain. Unlike many young people his age who left to join the freedom fighters, Andrew stays behind to support his father after his mother's death. This choice illustrates his sense of duty and responsibility, reflecting the broader impact of war on African families.

Family Dynamics

Andrew's strong bond with his older brother, Rwizi, emphasizes the familial duty in Shona tradition. However, his presence creates tension with Sally, who rejects African traditions, highlighting the cultural clash between traditional African values and Western influences.

Andrew's Courage and Outspokenness

Andrew demonstrates courage and assertiveness in standing up against Sally's oppressive and racist remarks. He challenges her views on the political and social situation in Rhodesia, showing his willingness to speak out against injustice and defend the rights of Africans.

Commitment to Cultural Heritage

Through his dialogue, Andrew displays a deep connection to his cultural heritage. He passionately argues for the value of African traditions and the importance of preserving their land and identity. This is evident when he talks about the history of Great Zimbabwe and the fraudulent Rudd Concession.

Political Awareness and Activism

Andrew's political awareness is highlighted as he critiques the colonial regime and its oppressive policies. He questions the legitimacy of the European presence in Africa and asserts the need for Africans to reclaim their land and rights.

Supportive and Protective

Andrew's interaction with John shows his protective nature. He is concerned about John's well-being at school and the racial bullying he faces. Despite Sally's unrealistic expectations of John to only speak English, Andrew teaches John the proper way to greet one's elders in Shona, something John should have to know how to do even though he may speak English.

5.   BELINDA

Belinda is a multifaceted character who embodies compassion, respect for tradition, practicality, and a strong moral compass. Her actions and interactions reveal her depth and complexity, making her a crucial figure in the narrative. Belinda's character highlights the importance of empathy, cultural respect, and moral integrity in maintaining healthy relationships and navigating complex social dynamics. Through Belinda, the play explores themes of cultural identity, family obligations, and the tension between tradition and modernity

Respectful and Culturally Conscious

Belinda shows deep respect for traditional African customs and values. She greets Majasi in a traditional Shona manner, clapping her hands and addressing him with respect. Her appreciation for African culture is further emphasized when she discusses the importance of "hunhu" and "ubuntu" for John's upbringing. Belinda emphasizes the need for cultural heritage alongside European education, contrasting with Sally's dismissive attitude towards African traditions

.

Practical and Thoughtful

Belinda's practical and reliable nature is evident in her actions. She ensures Sally has her umbrella for potential rain, brings sweets and biscuits for John and Majasi, and suggests remedies for Majasi's health issues. Her pragmatic approach ensures that her actions are considerate and beneficial for those she cares about.

Strong Moral Compass

A defining aspect of Belinda's character is her strong moral compass. She disapproves of Sally's actions, such as banishing her father-in-law to an old people's home and not informing Rwizi of his death. Belinda's strong sense of right and wrong drives her to provide honest and constructive advice, urging Sally to prioritize family over superficial social status. She is not afraid to speak her mind and challenge Sally's views, openly criticizing Sally's obsession with European culture and emphasizing the importance of African traditions.

Empathetic and Understanding

Belinda's empathy allows her to connect with others on a deeper level. She understands the cultural significance of mbira music and sympathizes with the loss of village life due to the war. Her empathetic nature makes her a comforting presence in the household, providing emotional support and understanding to those around her. She serves as a positive influence, encouraging John to take care of his grandfather and engaging in meaningful conversations about cultural heritage.

Honest and Direct

Belinda's honesty and directness highlight her integrity and willingness to stand up for what she believes is right. Despite her disapproval of Sally's actions, she remains a loyal and supportive friend, offering guidance and practical advice. Belinda's commitment to helping Sally make things right with Rwizi underscores her loyalty and sense of responsibility as a friend.

6. JOHN

John is an integral part of the play, which explores the era through the eyes of an innocent six-year-old boy caught between his African roots and his mother's aspiration for a European lifestyle. Despite his mother's intense efforts to have him live and act like a European, John remains largely oblivious to it, without being disrespectful to her.

John prefers to spend time with the other African children, whom his mother dismissively calls "those dirty children," instead of watching the white children who bully and racially marginalize him on a tv program. He has a natural affinity for his grandfather, Majasi, whose quiet dignity draws him in. John tells everyone, including his mother, that his grandfather is his best friend.

The close relationship between John and Majasi adds to Sally's urgency to send Majasi away from her house. John's heart is broken and he is left confused when he learns that his grandfather is dead. This deep bond and its subsequent disruption play a significant role in highlighting the cultural and generational conflicts within the story

Sheltered Upbringing

 John's mother, Sally, deliberately shields him from African traditions, immersing him in European culture. She enrolls him in an exclusive white school and prohibits the use of the Shona language in their home, grooming him to adopt a European identity and distancing him from his African heritage.

European Values

Sally's insistence on raising John with European values is evident in her choices, aiming to mold him into a European-cultured person. However,

John's experiences at school, where he is bullied and racially marginalized, contrast with his mother's intentions.

Cultural Conflict
John's upbringing places him at the center of the cultural conflict between his parents. While Sally promotes European culture, his father, Rwizi, and grandfather, Majasi, represent suppressed African traditions. John is caught between these conflicting cultural influences, trying to find his own identity.

Desire for Connection
Despite his sheltered upbringing, John wants to play with other African boys instead of the white children who bully him. This desire reflects his inherent connection to his African heritage and the struggle to balance his identity amidst external pressures,

7. BENJANI

Benjani, a young African houseboy in his twenties, works for Sally, wearing a coarse khaki uniform that signifies his lower social status. Despite limited English proficiency, he complies with Sally's rule against speaking Shona, showing his adaptability and adherence to employer demands. Benjani's respectful, deferential demeanor and diligent work reflect his position within the household hierarchy. His character embodies the struggles and strengths of domestic workers, navigating cultural and linguistic differences in a colonial setting. The play uses Benjani to explore themes of social hierarchy, cultural assimilation, and the challenges faced by those in servile positions.

8. CHAITEZVI

Chaitezvi, an elderly and traditional man, struggles to adapt to township life. Agitated by challenges such as his grandson's arrest and the lack of community support, he longs for the mutual assistance of his village. He represents the displacement felt by villagers seeking refuge in the township. Chaitezvi is grateful for the help from Andrew, Chamu, and Muchazo, recognizing the importance of community even in an urban setting. His character highlights the difficulties older generations face in adapting to new environments, emphasizing the significance of community, resourcefulness, and traditional values. Through him, the narrative explores generational differences, cultural heritage, and the need for mutual understanding across generations.

9.   CHAMU

Chamu is a humorous, intelligent, and pragmatic young man who uses humor to address serious topics, reflecting his awareness of Rhodesia's political and social challenges. Aspiring to be a lawyer, he is disillusioned by the turbulent socio-political climate and conscription threat. Chamu's resourcefulness and support for friends, seen in his encouragement of Andrew, demonstrate his commitment to their shared goals. His light-hearted demeanor makes difficult conversations approachable, and his resilience and determination highlight his willingness to pursue his passion for music despite oppression. Chamu's character embodies the strength and perseverance of Rhodesia's younger generation, exploring themes of aspiration, friendship, and resistance against oppression. Despite his playful nature, Chamu is insightful and aware of the political and social challenges in Rhodesia.

10.   MUCHAZO

Muchazo is a quiet, respectful, and empathetic young woman who embodies gentleness and kindness. Initially shy when Majasi jokes about her, her smile reveals warmth and friendliness. She is proactive and caring, as shown by her initiative to help Chaitezvi by involving neighbors and friendly policemen. Muchazo respects

African traditions, contrasting with Sally's rejection of them. As Andrew's supportive girlfriend, she plays a significant role in securing a job and dignified accommodation for his father. Her character highlights dedication to helping others, preserving cultural values, and the importance of community support in overcoming challenges. Through Muchazo, the play explores empathy, cultural heritage, and resilience.

B. CHARACTER RELATIONSHIPS

Relationships Between Characters in the Play

The relationships between the characters in the play are complex and multifaceted, reflecting the broader themes of cultural conflict, family obligations, and the struggle for identity. Each character's interactions and connections with others highlight the tensions and challenges of balancing tradition with modernity in a changing socio-political landscape. The inclusion of Belinda, Sam, Muchazo, Chamu, and Chaitezvi adds depth to the narrative, showcasing the diverse perspectives and experiences within the community.

Majasi

- **Father to Rwizi and Andrew**: Majasi is the elderly patriarch of the Choto family. He has a strong sense of duty and traditional values, having made sacrifices to ensure his children's education and well-being.

- **Father-in-law to Sally**: Majasi's presence in Rwizi's home creates tension with Sally, who rejects African traditions and views him as a disruption to her plans for raising their son with European values.
- **Grandfather to John**: Majasi's relationship with his grandson, John, is influenced by the cultural conflict between traditional African values and the European lifestyle that Sally aspires to.

Rwizi

- **Son to Majasi**: Rwizi feels a strong sense of duty to care for his elderly father, reflecting the traditional Shona values of family obligations and respect for elders.
- **Brother to Andrew**: Rwizi supports his younger brother, Andrew, by paying for his education and providing a home for him. Their relationship highlights the importance of family bonds and responsibilities.
- **Husband to Sally**: Rwizi's marriage to Sally is marked by cultural conflict, as he tries to balance his traditional responsibilities with Sally's desire for a European nuclear family lifestyle.
- **Father to John**: Rwizi is dedicated to raising his son, John, but faces challenges in reconciling his cultural heritage with Sally's aspirations for their son's upbringing.

Sally

- **Wife to Rwizi**: Sally's marriage to Rwizi is characterized by tension and conflict due to their differing cultural values. She rejects African traditions and insists on raising their son to be a European cultured person.
- **Daughter-in-law to Majasi**: Sally's relationship with Majasi is strained, as she views his presence in their home as a threat to her plans for their family's European lifestyle.

- **Mother to John**: Sally is determined to raise John with European values, enrolling him in an exclusive white school and forbidding him the use of the Shona language in their home.

Andrew

- **Son to Majasi**: Andrew respects his father and appreciates the sacrifices Majasi has made for his education and well-being.
- **Brother to Rwizi**: Andrew looks up to his older brother, Rwizi, and relies on him for support and guidance. Their relationship underscores the importance of family bonds and responsibilities.
- **Uncle to John**: Andrew's presence in the household creates tension with Sally, who views him as a disruption to her plans for raising John with European values.

John

- **Son to Rwizi and Sally**: John is a young and impressionable child caught in the cultural conflict between his parents. He is being raised to be a European cultured person, as per Sally's wishes, but is also influenced by his father's and grandfather's traditional African heritage.
- **Grandson to Majasi**: John's relationship with his grandfather, Majasi, is shaped by the cultural clash between traditional African values and the European lifestyle that Sally aspires to.
- **Nephew to Andrew**: John's interactions with his uncle, Andrew, further highlight the cultural conflict within the family.

Belinda

- **Friend to Sally**: Belinda is Sally's friend who respects and enjoys African customs and mbira music. Her acceptance and appreciation of African traditions create a contrast with Sally's rejection of her heritage.
- **Supportive Figure**: Belinda brings treats for John and Majasi, showing her acceptance and appreciation of African traditions. She serves as a supportive figure in the play, highlighting the possibility of cultural harmony.

Sam

- **Friend to Rwizi**: Sam is a friend of Rwizi who shares his political views and supports the liberation movements. Their friendship underscores the political undertones of the play and Rwizi's clandestine involvement in the struggle for independence.

Muchazo, Chamu, and The Band

- **Band Members and Friends to Andrew**: Muchazo, Chamu, and the mbira band are Andrew's friends and fellow band members. They share a strong bond through their love for mbira music and their shared experiences of displacement and uncertainty due to the war.
- **Cultural Connection**: Their involvement in mbira music gatherings highlights their connection to African traditions and their desire to preserve and celebrate their cultural heritage.

Chaitezvi

- **Neighbor and Community Member**: Chaitezvi is a neighbor who laments the absence of neighborly help in the city compared to the village. His character highlights the social isolation experienced by those who sought refuge in the townships and the challenges of maintaining community support in an urban environment.

Chapter 6

THEMES, MOTIFS AND SYMBOLS

THEMES and MOTIFS

CULTUTRAL CONFLICT

The play explores the clash between traditional extended family African values and the desire for European nuclear family cultural assimilation, embodied in Sally's rejection of her husband's family and traditions and her determination to raise her son as a "European." The presence of Majasi and Andrew, who bring the Shona language and mbira music, heightens the cultural tension. Set against the cultural and political tensions in 1970s Rhodesia, Sally's disdain for political meetings and the African liberation movement highlights the clash between the oppressed African majority and the white minority rule. Rwizi's clandestine support for the liberation movements underscores the widespread desire for independence. The tension between collective cultural heritage and personal aspirations is a central theme, illustrated by Sally's rejection of her aunt and her insistence on moving her father-in-law to Plumtree. Sally's party symbolizes her desire for social assimilation, contrasted by Andrew's arrival with tragic news. The recurring theme of cultural conflict is evident in Sally's determination to maintain a European lifestyle, her disdain for African traditions, and actions like sending Majasi to Plumtree, underscoring the complexities of identity and navigating a changing socio-political landscape.

FAMILY DUTY, LOYALTY & BETRAYAL
The play highlights the struggle of balancing familial responsibilities and personal ambitions through the character of Rwizi, who is caught between the demands of his nuclear family

and his extended family. Shona tradition dictates his duty to care for his father and brother, while Sally's expectations pressure him to conform to a European nuclear family lifestyle. This theme underscores the sacrifices and compromises required to fulfill familial obligations.

Andrew's accusation that Rwizi sent their father to his death in Plumtree illustrates the perceived betrayal of family responsibilities. Rwizi's emotional breakdown and plea for forgiveness from his deceased mother reflect the deep turmoil and guilt associated with neglecting these duties. Sally's actions, seen as a betrayal by Rwizi and Andrew, further highlight the consequences of prioritizing personal aspirations over family loyalty. The theme of family betrayal, duty, and loyalty is central to the narrative, emphasizing the emotional and ethical complexities of maintaining family bonds.

IDENTITY, ASSIMILLTION & SELF-DISCOVERY

The play examines the complexities of identity through Sally's efforts to distance herself from her African heritage and embrace European values. This desire for assimilation is symbolized by her ambitions in ballroom dancing and insistence on speaking English. The tension between maintaining cultural heritage and assimilating into a different culture is a central motif. Sally's determination to maintain a nuclear family lifestyle and her resistance to African traditions create household tension, emphasizing the struggle to reconcile cultural identities. Her internal conflict and the lengths she goes to maintain her constructed identity reflect the broader theme of identity and assimilation, exploring the impact of cultural assimilation on self-discovery and identity.

IMPACT OF WAR AND DISPLACEMENT

The play highlights the significant impact of the liberation war on African families. Majasi's displacement and the destruction of his home symbolize the broader suffering caused by the conflict, disrupting the Choto family's stability and forcing them to navigate new social dynamics. Recurring themes include Majasi's displacement, Andrew's struggle to find employment, and the economic sanctions affecting the country, illustrating the broader consequences of the war. The desire for vengeance and the decision to stay and care for family members underscore the personal toll of the war on the characters.

SOCIAL STATUS AND ASPIRATIONS: A PRECIS
Sally's pursuit of social status and recognition within the white ruling moneyed society is a recurring motif. Her desire to host the ballroom dancing club's after-party and be seen in society pages reflects her aspiration to be part of the upper middle class. This theme underscores the sacrifices and compromises made in the quest for social mobility. Sally's actions, driven by a need to maintain appearances and achieve recognition, highlight the tension between personal ambition and collective obligations. Her obsession with social status leads to morally questionable decisions, such as hiding Majasi's death, to ensure her party's success. The play emphasizes the emotional and ethical complexities of maintaining social status and the impact on family and cultural responsibilities.

MUSIC AS A CULTURAL SYMBOL
Music plays a symbolic role in the play, representing the cultural clash between African and European identities. Mbira music signifies the connection to African heritage, while ballroom dancing to European music symbolizes the aspiration for assimilation. The mbira sessions and Andrew's involvement with the band highlight the preservation of cultural identity and resistance. The contrast between traditional mbira music and Sally's ballroom dancing aspirations underscores the cultural divide within the family. This motif emphasizes the tension between preserving cultural heritage and assimilating into a dominant culture.

GENERATIONAL DIFFERENCES AND OBLIGATIONS

The play underscores the challenges of maintaining cultural continuity across generations within the Choto family. Majasi's adherence to traditional values contrasts with Sally's modern aspirations, creating conflicting expectations for Rwizi. Andrew represents the younger generation caught between these influences, while six-year-old John is being raised in a sheltered environment with European values, adding another layer to the cultural conflict. The need for mutual understanding and support across generations is emphasized. The contrasting reactions to Majasi's death highlight the generational divide, with Sally's detachment from traditional values contrasting sharply with Rwizi and Andrew's connection to cultural heritage and familial duty. This theme explores the complexities of fulfilling family obligations while navigating personal aspirations and societal pressures.

LOVE, FRIENDHSHIP & SUPPORT
The play highlights the importance of love and friendship through various relationships. The budding romance between Andrew and Muchazo, along with the supportive friendship within the mbira band, adds warmth and hope to the narrative. Majasi's friendship with Chaitezvi and Belinda's support for Rwizi highlight the significance of companionship and mutual support in challenging circumstances. These relationships underscore the significance of companionship and mutual support in challenging circumstances. Muchazo's efforts to find Andrew a job and a home for his father emphasize community support. Additionally, the bond between Rwizi and Andrew, despite tensions, and John's choice to stay with his father and uncle, illustrate the family's solidarity and commitment to navigating difficult circumstances together.

IMPACT OF TRAUMA AND PAST
Sally's anger towards her aunt reveals deep-seated trauma from her past, shaping her attitudes and actions. Her mother's banishment and the subsequent struggles have left Sally determined to distance herself from anything that reminds her of her African heritage. This motif underscores the long-lasting

impact of personal and generational trauma on individuals and their relationships

RESISTANCE AND LIBERATION

The play highlights the theme of resistance against oppression through a political meeting disguised as a traditional mbira gathering and Andrew's encounter with freedom fighters. The liberation movement's impact on the characters' lives underscores the collective struggle for independence and the personal sacrifices involved. Andrew's decision to join the freedom fighters symbolizes his shift from seeking personal safety to actively participating in the fight for liberation.

GRIEF AND MOURNING

The theme of grief and mourning is poignantly depicted through Rwizi's emotional breakdown and John's confusion over Majasi's death. The juxtaposition of the celebratory party and the mourning on the veranda highlights the family's emotional distress and the contrast between public appearances and private suffering. Majasi's loss of his wife, killed by Rhodesian soldiers, and the destruction of his home force him to navigate his grief in Beatrice Cottage. This personal tragedy, compounded by displacement and struggle to adapt, underscores the profound impact on the family. The play emphasizes the personal and collective toll of mourning within the family.

RACISM AND APARTHEID

The play explores the theme of racism and apartheid on individual and societal levels. Six-year-old John faces bullying at school by his white classmates, reflecting pervasive racism in Rhodesian society. This bullying highlights systemic discrimination against black Africans. John's struggles mirror the broader apartheid system, perpetuating inequality and segregation. The Choto family's experiences emphasize the deep-seated racial tensions and challenges of maintaining cultural identity. Despite pervasive racism, the characters demonstrate resilience and resistance, supported by family and community solidarity. The play underscores the enduring fight for equality and justice amidst systemic discrimination.

PERFORMANCE AND IDENTITY

The play intricately weaves themes of performance and identity, illustrating characters navigating their cultural identities through various performances. The themes of performance and identity explore the complexities of navigating cultural identities amidst a changing socio-political landscape, highlighting characters' struggles with assimilation, resistance, and cultural preservation.

1. Ballroom Dancing: Sally's ballroom dancing symbolizes her aspiration for colonial respectability and social assimilation. This drive leads her to meticulously curate her public image, often at the expense of her cultural heritage and familial duties.

2. Political Meetings as Disguised Gatherings: Political meetings disguised as Shona bira gatherings highlight resistance against oppression. These covert performances blend cultural rituals with political activism, showcasing the resilience of the African community.

3. Sally's Curation of Public Image: Sally's careful curation of her public image reflects her struggle with identity and assimilation, maintaining a European facade and disdain for African traditions, emphasizing the pressures of cultural assimilation.

4. Mbira Music and Cultural Expression: The mbira music performance by Andrew, Chamu, and Muchazo before delivering news symbolizes the preservation of cultural heritage and emotional expression. This juxtaposition underscores the interconnectedness of cultural identity and personal experiences.

SYMBOLIC ELEMENTS IN THEMES AND MOTIFS

SALLY'S BALLROOM GOWN

Sally's ballroom gown symbolizes her aspiration for colonial respectability and social assimilation, reflecting her desire to be accepted within European society.

THE BAR IN RWIZI'S HOUSE

- Symbol of Affluence: The bar represents the family's wealth and social status.
- Privilege: During the Rhodesia - Ian Smith era, Africans were excluded from white-only bars that served cocktails, often only able to access cheap opaque beers. Rwizi and Sally having a bar and making cocktails at home highlights their significant social elevation and the symbolism of overcoming racial barriers.

THE RADIO

Mbira music playing on the radio in Sally's house in Majasi's presence serves as a powerful symbol of cultural resilience, generational conflict, emotional refuge, silent defiance, and intergenerational bonding within the narrative.

THE TV

The television represents the influence of Western culture and the allure of European lifestyles, contributing to the characters' internal conflicts with their cultural identities.

THE MBIRA

THE MBIRA is a cultural symbol of African heritage and traditions, representing the characters' connection to their roots and the preservation of their cultural identity amidst external pressures.

THE TWO PAPER BAGS

In the final scenes, Andrew arrives with two brown paper bags:

- One containing his father's effects, symbolizing tradition and family.
- One containing a bomb, representing political resistance.
- The moment when he must choose which to protect represents the impossible choices faced by young Africans, torn between family loyalty and political activism.

THE TROPHY

The ballroom dancing trophy symbolizes:

- Empty Colonial Aspiration: The pursuit of validation through colonial institutions.
- Cultural Betrayal: The cost of abandoning one's cultural heritage for superficial achievements.
- Futility: The ultimate meaninglessness of seeking approval from oppressive structures.

THE HAT

Belinda's gift of a hat to Majasi, which she later plans to place on his coffin, represents:

- Bridging Cultural Divides: The possibility of reconciliation between different cultural values.
- Respect for Traditional Values: Honoring cultural heritage within modern life.
- Personal Cost: The emotional and cultural toll of Sally's rejection of her heritage.

These symbolic elements collectively emphasize the play's exploration of cultural identity, resistance, and the complexities of navigating a racially and politically divided society.

THEMES AND MOTIFS: STYLE & STRUCTURE

Use of Space

The play uses domestic space to represent larger political conflicts:

- <u>The Living Room</u>: Represents a battlefield between musical traditions, symbolizing the clash between African heritage and European aspirations.
- <u>The Veranda</u>: Serves as a liminal space between public and private, highlighting the tension between personal identity and societal expectations.
- <u>The Physical Distance to Plumtree</u>: Represents cultural distance, underscoring the challenges of reconciling traditional values with modern aspirations.

LANGUAGE AND MUSIC

The play employs multiple registers of language and music to illustrate the characters' struggles with identity and cultural heritage:

- <u>English versus Shona</u>: Highlights the tension between assimilation into European society and the preservation of African identity.
- <u>Classical European versus Traditional African Music</u>: Reflects the cultural clash and the characters' efforts to navigate their identities within these contrasting influences.
- <u>The Battle Over John's Language Development</u>: Emphasizes the ongoing struggle to maintain cultural heritage amidst pressures to conform to dominant societal norms.

These stylistic and structural elements enhance the play's exploration of cultural conflict, identity, and the impact of socio-political dynamics on personal lives.

Chapter 7

LITERARY DEVICES

The authour's use of language and style in this play is both vivid and evocative, effectively capturing the socio-political landscape of Rhodesia in 1977. The narrative is rich in detail, providing a comprehensive backdrop that immerses the reader in the setting and the lives of the characters.

Language

- <u>Descriptive and Detailed</u>: The authour employs descriptive language to paint a clear picture of the setting and characters. For example, the description of Beatrice Cottages and the National African Township provides a stark contrast between different living conditions.
- <u>Cultural References</u>: The use of Shona terms and references to African traditions and customs adds authenticity and depth to the narrative. This helps to ground the story in its cultural context and provides insight into the characters' backgrounds and beliefs.
- <u>Dialogue</u>: The dialogue is natural and reflective of the characters' personalities and social standings. The use of broken English by Benjani, for instance, highlights his lower social status and the language barriers he faces.

Style

- <u>Realism</u>: The play adopts a realistic style, portraying the everyday lives and struggles of the Choto family. This slice-of-life approach allows the audience to connect with the characters on a personal level.
- <u>Conflict and Tension</u>: The authour builds conflict and tension through the interactions between characters, particularly between Sally and Rwizi. Sally's disdain for African traditions and her obsession with European culture create a palpable tension that drives the narrative forward.

- Symbolism: The play uses symbolism to convey deeper meanings. For example, the ballroom dancing represents Sally's aspiration for a European lifestyle, while the mbira music symbolizes the traditional African heritage that she rejects.
- Characterization: The authour provides detailed characterizations, allowing the audience to understand the motivations and conflicts of each character. Sally's background as an orphan and her determination to raise her son as a European are key to understanding her actions and attitudes.

Overall, the authour's use of language and style effectively brings the story to life, providing a rich and immersive experience that highlights the cultural and social dynamics of Rhodesia in 1977.

FIGURATIVE LANGUAGE AND THEIR EFFECTS

1. **Metaphor**: "The play is a slice of life in Rhodesia circa 1977."
   - **Effect**: This metaphor sets the tone for the play, indicating that it provides a realistic and detailed portrayal of everyday life in Rhodesia during that time period.
2. **Metaphor**: "Sally suddenly finds her carefully manicured nuclear family life being invaded by the pestilence of her husband's family from the African reservation villages."
   - **Effect**: The metaphor "pestilence" conveys Sally's negative perception of her husband's family, suggesting that she views their presence as a harmful and unwelcome intrusion into her orderly life.
3. **Simile**: "Sally is aghast that her husband would forego going to a ballroom dancing practice session to spend time attending useless meetings with 'uneducated Africans howling at the moon and clamoring for independence from their white benefactors'."

- o **Effect**: The simile "howling at the moon" emphasizes Sally's disdain for the political meetings and her condescending attitude towards the African liberation movements, portraying them as futile and irrational.

4. **Hyperbole**: "Sally threatens to leave him with their son, if he does not comply with that demand before the ballroom dancing competition date."
   - o **Effect**: This hyperbole highlights the intensity of Sally's ultimatum and her determination to maintain her desired lifestyle, even at the cost of her marriage.

5. **Imagery**: "The meeting, held under the guise of a native Shona traditional ancestral mbira music bhira (gathering) is attended by a mix of young and older men and women with men, including Rwizi, adorning animal fur hats on their heads and the women wearing wraparound colored cloth around their waists, as a political statement."
   - o **Effect**: The vivid imagery in this description paints a clear picture of the cultural and political significance of the gathering, emphasizing the characters' connection to their heritage and their resistance to colonial rule.

6. **Symbolism**: "At the center of their social life is ballroom dancing to classical European music."
   - o **Effect**: Ballroom dancing symbolizes Sally's aspiration for a European lifestyle and her desire to distance herself from traditional African culture. It represents the cultural conflict at the heart of the play.

These examples of figurative language enhance the narrative by adding depth to the characters' emotions and perspectives, creating a more engaging and immersive experience for the audience

DRAMATIC TECHNIQUE

The authour uses several dramatic techniques to enhance the storytelling and convey the themes of the play effectively, such as::

1. Symbolism

- **Mbira Music vs. European Classical Music**: The contrast between mbira music and European classical music symbolizes the cultural conflict between traditional African values and European assimilation. Mbira music represents African tradition, language, and community, while European classical music embodies a different cultural identity.

2. Characterization

- **Complex Characters**: The authour creates multi-dimensional characters with distinct personalities, backgrounds, and motivations. Characters like Majasi, Rwizi, Sally, and Andrew each represent different aspects of the cultural and socio-political landscape, allowing the audience to explore various perspectives.

3. Conflict

- **Cultural and Political Conflict**: The play is driven by both cultural and political conflicts. The tension between traditional African values and European assimilation is a central theme, as is the political struggle for liberation from white minority rule.
- **Interpersonal Conflict**: The authour uses interpersonal conflicts, such as the tension between Sally and Majasi, to highlight broader societal issues and the impact of cultural differences on personal relationships.

4. Flashbacks

- **Revealing Backstory**: The use of flashbacks helps to reveal the characters' past experiences and traumas, providing context for their actions and motivations. For example, Sally's traumatic childhood is revealed through flashbacks, explaining her rejection of African traditions.

5. Dialogue

- **Authentic Conversations**: The authour uses dialogue to convey the characters' emotions, thoughts, and cultural backgrounds. The conversations between characters are authentic and reflect the complexities of their relationships and the socio-political environment.
- **Language**: The use of both English and Shona languages in the dialogue highlights the cultural conflict and the characters' struggles with identity and assimilation.

6. Setting

- **Contrasting Environments**: The play's setting contrasts the rural village life with the urban environment of Beatrice Cottages. This contrast underscores the impact of the war and the displacement experienced by the characters.
- **Historical Context**: The setting during the war of liberation provides a historical backdrop that influences the characters' actions and the overall narrative.

7. Symbolic Actions

- **Ballroom Dancing**: Sally's participation in ballroom dancing symbolizes her desire to assimilate into European culture and distance herself from her African heritage. This symbolic action highlights the cultural conflict within the play.

8. Themes

- **Cultural Assimilation and Identity**: The play explores the tension between traditional African values and the desire to assimilate into European culture. This theme is central to the characters' struggles and conflicts.

- **Family Obligations and Loyalty**: The play examines the responsibilities and duties within a family, particularly the expectations placed on the eldest son, Rwizi, to care for his relatives.
- **Social Status and Class**: The Choto family's social standing and their aspirations for a higher status are central to the narrative, highlighting the pressures and sacrifices made to achieve and maintain social status.
- **Political and Social Change**: Set against the backdrop of the Rhodesian Bush War, the play addresses the broader socio-political dynamics of the time and the impact of the war on the family's life.

These dramatic techniques work together to create a rich and engaging narrative that captures the complexities of cultural assimilation, family dynamics, and socio-political change.

Chapter 8

1. What is the mbira and its significance in the play?

The mbira is a traditional Zimbabwean musical instrument, often (erroneously)referred to as a "thumb piano", consisting of metal tines attached to a wooden board. It holds significant cultural and spiritual importance in Zimbabwe, serving as a medium for communication with ancestral spirits and as a symbol of cultural identity. In "*High Class Natives: The Ballroom Dancers & Mbira Players,*" the mbira plays a crucial role in highlighting the themes of cultural conflict, identity, and resistance against colonial oppression.

Significance of the Mbira in the Play

CULTURAL IDENTITY AND HERITAGE

The mbira symbolizes traditional African culture and serves as a reminder of the rich heritage that characters like Andrew strive to connect with. As Andrew engages with mbira players, he embodies the struggle to reclaim cultural identity amidst the pressures of colonial assimilation represented by Sally's preference for European ballroom dancing. This connection to the mbira reflects a deeper yearning for authenticity and belonging within a society that often marginalizes traditional practices.

RESISTANCE AGAINST COLONIAL INFLUENCE

The presence of mbira music in the play acts as a form of resistance against the cultural erasure imposed by colonialism. While Sally seeks to distance her family from their African roots, Andrew's involvement with mbira players signifies a rejection of this assimilationist attitude. The mbira becomes a tool for expressing defiance against colonial oppression, reinforcing the idea that traditional culture can serve as a source of strength and resilience.

SYMBOL OF UNITY AND COMMUNITY

The mbira also represents community and unity among those who embrace their cultural heritage. In contrast to Sally's isolationist tendencies, Andrew's participation in mbira music fosters connections with others who share similar values and experiences. This communal aspect highlights the importance of collective identity in resisting colonial narratives and maintaining cultural practices.

MUSICAL METAPHOR FOR CONFLICT

The interplay between mbira music and ballroom dancing serves as a metaphor for the broader cultural conflict within the play. While ballroom dancing symbolizes colonial aspirations and social mobility, the mbira embodies indigenous traditions and resistance. The inability of these musical forms to coexist peacefully within the Choto household mirrors the larger societal tensions between Western influence and African heritage.

PERSONAL CONNECTION TO ANCESTRY

For characters like Andrew, playing the mbira is not just an act of musical expression but also a way to connect with their ancestors and cultural roots. This personal connection emphasizes the spiritual significance of the mbira, illustrating how music can serve as a bridge between generations and foster a sense of continuity in the face of disruption caused by war and colonialism.

In "High Class Natives," the mbira serves as a powerful symbol of cultural identity, resistance, community, and ancestral connection. Its significance extends beyond mere musicality; it encapsulates the struggles faced by characters navigating their identities within a colonial context. Through the contrasting representations of ballroom dancing and mbira music, the authour poignantly illustrates the complexities of cultural conflict and the enduring power of traditional heritage in shaping individual and collective identities.

In summary, the mbira serves as a vital bridge for social cohesion in "High Class Natives: The Ballroom Dancers & Mbira Players," facilitating connections among characters and fostering community ties

2. Explore the concept of The Mbira as a Bridge for Social Cohesion

CULTURAL CONNECTION
The mbira represents a deep-rooted cultural heritage that resonates with the characters, particularly Andrew. As he engages with the mbira players, he finds common ground with Muchazo and others who share a passion for this traditional instrument. This shared interest fosters camaraderie and friendship, allowing them to bond over their collective appreciation of African culture.

COMMUNITY BUILDING
Through the act of playing the mbira, characters come together in a communal setting that transcends individual struggles. The music creates a space where cultural identity is celebrated, reinforcing social bonds among those who participate. This communal aspect is essential in a society marked by colonial oppression, where traditional practices serve as a source of resilience and unity.

RESISTANCE AGAINST ALIENATION
In contrast to Sally's attempts to distance her family from their African roots through ballroom dancing, the mbira symbolizes resistance against cultural alienation. By embracing mbira music, Andrew and Muchazo assert their identities and challenge the colonial narrative that seeks to erase their heritage. This act of

cultural affirmation strengthens their friendship and reinforces their connection to their community.

SHARED PASSION AND FRIENDSHIP

The relationship between Andrew and Muchazo is significantly shaped by their mutual love for the mbira. This shared passion not only brings them closer but also highlights the importance of cultural practices in forging friendships. Their connection through music allows them to navigate the complexities of their identities within a colonial context, providing emotional support and solidarity.

SYMBOL OF HOPE AND RESILIENCE

When Andrew finds his father dead in Plumtree, it is through the mbira that he finds solace and strength. The mbira transcends mere musicality; it embodies hope and resilience in the face of adversity. As characters gather around the mbira, they create an atmosphere of joy and solidarity that counters the oppressive realities of their lives. This sense of community becomes crucial for psychological survival amidst the turmoil of war and societal change.

In "High Class Natives," the mbira serves as a powerful symbol of social cohesion, bringing characters together through shared cultural practices and fostering friendships rooted in mutual appreciation for their heritage. By highlighting the significance of the mbirathe authour underscores the importance of traditional culture as a means of resistance against colonial oppression and as a foundation for community solidarity. The relationships formed through this shared passion illustrate how music can bridge divides, create connections, and nurture resilience within a fragmented society.

1. How does the setting of Beatrice Cottages influence the characters' behaviours?

The setting of Beatrice Cottages plays a crucial role in shaping the characters' behaviors and interactions in "High Class Natives: The Ballroom Dancers & Mbira Players." Here are several ways in which this setting influences the characters:

SOCIO-ECONOMIC CONTEXT

Upper Middle-Class Aspirations: Beatrice Cottages is depicted as a residential area that is a step above typical African housing during the late 1970s in Rhodesia. This status influences Rwizi and Sally's aspirations to maintain an upper-middle-class lifestyle, which drives their desire to project a certain image to their peers. Sally's insistence on raising their son, John, to embody European cultural values reflects her attempts to align their family with the social status associated with living in Beatrice Cottages.

CULTURAL TENSIONS

Cultural Clashes: The juxtaposition of European ballroom dancing and traditional mbira music within the same household creates significant tension. Sally's disdain for her in-laws' traditional values and practices is exacerbated by their presence in her home, which she perceives as a threat to her carefully curated lifestyle. The setting amplifies these cultural conflicts, as the physical space of the home becomes a battleground for competing cultural identities.

FAMILY DYNAMICS

Generational Conflicts: The presence of Majasi (Rwizi's father) and Andrew (Rwizi's younger brother) in the household brings generational conflicts to the forefront. Rwizi feels a sense of duty to care for his family, reflecting traditional African values, while

Sally prioritizes her personal aspirations. This dynamic is intensified by the setting, as the confined space of Beatrice Cottages forces these differing values into direct confrontation.

POLITICAL CLIMATE
Impact of War: The backdrop of political unrest and liberation movements influence character behavior significantly. Rwizi's involvement in political meetings reflects a response to the societal pressures of living under colonial rule. The setting serves as a reminder of the external political turmoil that seeps into their daily lives, affecting decisions and relationships within the household.

ISOLATION VS. COMMUNITY
Social Isolation: While Beatrice Cottages offers a semblance of comfort and status, it also isolates Rwizi and Sally from their cultural roots and broader community ties. Sally's attempts to distance herself from her husband's family highlight this isolation, as she seeks to create a life that aligns with her European aspirations while neglecting her African heritage.

CONCLUSION
The setting of Beatrice Cottages is not just a backdrop but an active participant in the narrative, influencing character motivations, relationships, and conflicts. It encapsulates the struggles between tradition and modernity, family loyalty and personal ambition, reflecting the broader societal changes occurring during this tumultuous period in Rhodesia.

4. What are the main themes explored in "High Class Natives"

CULTURAL IDENTITY AND CONFLICT

The play highlights the clash between traditional African culture and Western influences. The characters navigate their identities through the contrasting symbols of European ballroom dancing and traditional mbira music. This cultural dichotomy manifests in the family dynamics, particularly between Rwizi, who feels torn between his African heritage and his wife Sally's aspirations for a Westernized nuclear family lifestyle.

FAMILY DYNAMICS AND OBLIGATIONS

Family loyalty is a central theme, as Rwizi struggles to balance his responsibilities to his father, Majasi, and brother, Andrew, with his obligations to his wife and son. The tensions arising from these conflicting loyalties illustrate the pressures faced by individuals in maintaining familial bonds while pursuing personal ambitions.

POLITICAL STRUGGLE AND ACTIVISM

Set against the backdrop of the liberation movement in Rhodesia, the play addresses themes of political resistance and social justice. Rwizi's clandestine support for liberation movements contrasts with Sally's dismissive attitude towards political activism. This divergence reflects broader societal attitudes toward colonial rule and the fight for independence.

SOCIOECONOMIC ASPIRATIONS

The characters' aspirations for upward mobility are evident in their desire to conform to middle-class standards. Sally's determination to raise their son as a "European" symbolizes the internalized colonial mindset and the desire for acceptance within a racially stratified society. This theme underscores the impact of socioeconomic status on personal relationships and cultural identity.

GENERATIONAL DIVIDE

The interactions between different generations within the Choto family reveal a generational divide regarding cultural values and political engagement. Majasi represents traditional wisdom and values, while Andrew embodies youthful rebellion and a desire for change. This theme emphasizes the evolving nature of cultural identity amidst societal transformation.

CONCLUSION
Through its exploration of these themes, "High Class Natives" offers a nuanced commentary on the complexities of identity, culture, and politics in Rhodesia during a time of significant upheaval. The interplay between personal aspirations and cultural heritage serves as a poignant reflection on the challenges faced by individuals navigating their identities in a changing world.

5. What role does the houseboy, Benjani, play in the narrative?

In "High Class Natives: The Ballroom Dancers & Mbira Players," the character of Benjani, the houseboy, plays a multifaceted role that significantly contributes to the narrative's exploration of themes such as class, cultural identity, and family dynamics.

Role of Benjani in the Narrative

SYMBOL OF CLASS STRUCTURE
Benjani represents the servant class within the socio-economic hierarchy of Rhodesia during the late 1970s. His presence in the Choto household underscores the disparities between the upper-middle-class aspirations of Rwizi and Sally and the realities of their cultural heritage. As a houseboy, who can barely speak the English his employer(Sally) demands of him, Benjani's role highlights the complexities of class relations in a society grappling with colonial legacies.

CULTURAL BRIDGE
Benjani serves as a cultural intermediary between the traditional African values embodied by Majasi and Andrew and the Westernized lifestyle that Sally aspires to maintain. His interactions with other characters often reflect the tensions between these two worlds, providing insights into how cultural identity is negotiated within the household.

CATALYST FOR CONFLICT
His presence can also act as a catalyst for conflict, especially in relation to Sally's disdain for traditional African customs. As she attempts to distance her family from their African roots, Benjani's role as a servant who embodies those very traditions creates friction within the family dynamic. This tension is particularly

evident when Sally's aspirations clash with her husband's obligations to his family.

OBSERVER OF FAMILY DYNAMICS

Benjani often serves as an observer and commentator on the events unfolding within the Choto household. His perspective can provide a unique lens through which audiences can understand the underlying tensions and conflicts among family members, particularly regarding issues of loyalty, tradition, and modernity.

REFLECTION OF SOCIETAL CHANGES

As Rhodesia undergoes significant political and social changes during this period, Benjani's character reflects broader societal shifts. His experiences and interactions with other characters can illustrate how ordinary people navigate these changes, providing a microcosm of the larger struggles faced by individuals in a transforming society.

CONCLUSION

Benjani's role in "High Class Natives" is essential for understanding the interplay of class, culture, and familial obligations within the narrative. Through his character the authour effectively explores themes of identity and conflict that resonate throughout the play, enriching the audience's comprehension of the characters' struggles against their socio-political backdrop.

6. Detail the importance of differentiating major and minor characters analyzing a play.

Differentiating between major and minor characters in a play is crucial for a comprehensive analysis, as it allows for a deeper understanding of the narrative's structure, themes, and character dynamics. Here's an exploration of the importance of this differentiation, particularly in the context of "High Class Natives: Ballroom Dancers & Mbira Players" by Alf E.F. Muronda.

Understanding Character Development

MAJOR CHARACTERS

These characters, such as Rwizi, Sally, and Majasi, are central to the plot and undergo significant development throughout the play. Their motivations, conflicts, and transformations drive the narrative forward. For instance, Rwizi's struggle to balance his traditional obligations with his aspirations for success illustrates the broader theme of cultural conflict.

MINOR CHARACTERS

Characters like Muchazo and Belinda serve to support and enhance the main themes without being the focus of the narrative. Their interactions with major characters provide insights into the primary conflicts. For example, Muchazo's connection to mbira music highlights the cultural resistance against colonial influences, enriching the play's exploration of identity.

Highlighting Themes and Motifs

THEMATIC EXPLORATION

Major characters often embody the central themes of the play. Rwizi's internal conflict between family loyalty and personal ambition reflects themes of cultural identity and familial obligation. In contrast, minor characters can represent specific aspects of these themes. For example, Belinda's successful navigation between African and colonial cultures serves as a counterpoint to Sally's rejection of her heritage.

SYMBOLIC ROLES

Minor characters can also serve symbolic functions that reinforce thematic elements. For instance, Muchazo's friendship with Andrew through their shared passion for mbira music emphasizes community cohesion and cultural pride, contrasting sharply with Sally's isolationist tendencies.

Character Relationships and Dynamics

INTERPERSONAL CONFLICTS

The interactions between major and minor characters reveal underlying tensions within the family and society. The conflicts between Sally (a major character) and Andrew (a minor character) regarding cultural values illustrate generational divides in attitudes towards tradition versus modernity.

SUPPORTIVE ROLES

Minor characters often provide essential support to major characters' arcs. For example, Andrew's relationship with Muchazo showcases how shared cultural practices can foster friendships that transcend family conflicts, highlighting the importance of community in navigating personal struggles.

Narrative Structure and Focus

PLOT ADVANCEMENT

Major characters typically drive the plot through their decisions and actions. Their journeys are crucial for understanding the play's trajectory. For example, Rwizi's secret support for liberation movements adds layers to his character while propelling the narrative towards its climax.

CONTEXTUALIZING EVENTS

Minor characters help contextualize events within the play without overshadowing major plotlines. Their presence enriches the world-building by providing background perspectives or commentary on significant events.

Emotional Resonance

AUDIENCE CONNECTION

Major characters often evoke stronger emotional responses from the audience due to their depth and complexity. Their struggles resonate on a personal level, making their journeys impactful. In contrast, minor characters can evoke empathy or reflection through their interactions with major characters.

CONTRASTING EXPERIENCES

The juxtaposition of major and minor characters allows for a richer emotional landscape. For instance, while Rwizi grapples with his identity amidst societal pressures, minor characters like Andrew can reflect youthful optimism or disillusionment in response to similar challenges.

CONCLUSION

Differentiating between major and minor characters is essential for analyzing "High Class Natives." This distinction helps illuminate character development, thematic depth, interpersonal dynamics, narrative structure, and emotional resonance within the play. By understanding how each character contributes to the overarching narrative, readers can gain a more nuanced appreciation of Muronda's exploration of cultural identity, familial obligation, and resistance against colonial oppression in late 1970s Rhodesia.

Chapter 9

GENERAL EXAMINATION RESOURCES

Examination Approaches
- When writing about the play, consider:
- How music and dance function as both literal and metaphorical elements.
- The relationship between personal tragedy and national conflict.
- The role of traditional culture in political resistance.
- The impact of colonialism on family structures.
- Various forms of performance in colonial society.
- Treatment of space as metaphor for cultural boundaries.

Contextual Reading
- Consider reading alongside:
- Historical accounts from late 1970s Rhodesia.
- Theories on cultural hybridity and postcolonialism.
- Studies on African traditional music and dance.

Practice Questions
Analyze how the authour uses music and dance to explore cultural conflict.

Discuss significance of space within familial relationships in the play.

Compare Sally's approach to that of Belinda regarding their identities within colonial society.

Examine how traditional culture serves as a form of

Additional Resources and Texts Complementing "High Class Natives"
To enhance the understanding and appreciation of Alf E.F. Muronda's "High Class Natives," it is beneficial to explore other

literary works that address similar themes of identity, colonialism, and cultural conflict within the Zimbabwean context and beyond. Below is a curated list of texts and resources that can serve as complementary readings.

Zimbabwean Literature

"Nervous Conditions" by Tsitsi Dangarembga This seminal novel explores the struggles of a young Shona girl, Tambu, as she navigates the challenges of gender and colonial education. It provides insights into the complexities of identity and the impact of colonialism on personal aspirations.

"The House of Hunger" by Dambudzo Marechera A collection of interconnected stories that vividly portray life in Zimbabwe during and after colonial rule. Marechera's work is known for its raw emotional power and critique of societal norms.

"The Stone Virgins" by Yvonne Vera This novel delves into the Gukurahundi massacres in Zimbabwe, exploring themes of trauma, loss, and resilience through the eyes of two sisters. Vera's poetic style offers a profound reflection on national identity and historical memory.

"We Need New Names" by NoViolet Bulawayo A coming-of-age story that follows a young girl named Darling as she experiences life in both Zimbabwe and America. The novel addresses issues of displacement, cultural identity, and the immigrant experience.

"House of Stone" by Novuyo Rosa Tshuma This novel weave together personal narratives against the backdrop of Zimbabwe's tumultuous history, particularly focusing on the Gukurahundi massacres. It examines themes of loss, belonging, and the search for truth.

Plays and Drama

"Death and the King's Horseman" by Wole Soyinka   A classic African play that explores cultural conflicts between colonial powers and indigenous traditions. It raises questions about duty, honor, and the consequences of cultural misunderstanding.

"Woza Albert!" by Percy Mtwa, Mbongeni Ngema, and Barney Simon A powerful political satire that critiques apartheid in South Africa while resonating with broader themes of oppression and resistance relevant to Zimbabwean history.
"
Anowa" by Ama Ata Aidoo This play addresses gender roles within traditional African society while exploring themes of autonomy and cultural expectations. It serves as a poignant commentary on women's struggles in post-colonial contexts.

Scholarly Resources

"Contemporary African Plays" edited by Martin Banham and Jane Plastow
This anthology includes significant plays from various African playwrights, providing context for understanding contemporary issues in African theatre. The collection highlights diverse voices and perspectives on post-colonial identity.

"The Postcolonial Studies Reader" edited by Bill Ashcroft, Gareth Griffiths, and Helen Tiffin
This comprehensive resource offers critical essays on postcolonial theory that can help frame discussions around "High Class Natives," particularly in relation to identity formation in post-colonial societies.

Historical Literature

Rhodesian Bush War (1965-1979) Decolonization and the Fight for Zimbabwean Independence By Daniel Wrinn

www.ingramcontent.com/pod-product-compliance
Lightning Source LLC
Chambersburg PA
CBHW041144120626
46547CB00020B/3098